INANE BALDERDASH

ASSEMBLED WORKS 2009

DAVID Q. TAGUE

iUniverse, Inc.
New York   Bloomington

Inane Balderdash

iUniverse books may be ordered through booksellers or by contacting:

iUniverse
1663 Liberty Drive
Bloomington, IN 47403
www.iuniverse.com
1-800-Authors (1-800-288-4677)

ISBN: 978-1-4401-3820-1 (sc)
ISBN: 978-1-4401-3821-8 (ebook)

Printed in the United States of America

iUniverse rev. date: 04/29/2009

"Imagine all the people, sharing all the world."

—J. Lennon

"Take a sad song, and make it better."

—P. McCartney

"The farther one travels, the less one knows."

—G. Harrison

"It don't come easy."

—R. Starkey

CONTENTS

PREFACE

Dearest Reader;

Hello and welcome to my second collection of prose, poetry, and useless piffle.

If you have not read my first book, *Miscellaneous Hullabaloo*, that's quite all right.

You see, technically, I hadn't originally intended on putting together this particular cacophony of chaotic conundrum. But, since you now hold it in your hands, you can read this one *first*, and then treat yourself to the first book *next*. In fact, you may very well *need to*.

Using age forty as a cut-off point, I prefer to refer to the man I used to be for the first thirty-nine years of my life as a *Former Version of Myself*.

For many years, this F.V.O.M. (abbreviated to save ink and simultaneously hold your interest, which is now waning since I chose to explain why in a lengthy parenthetical addendum) suffered from a malady that has yet to make it's way into the *Diagnostic Criteria From DSM-IV-TR™*. It is a state of mind that persists to exist until *Reality* eventually invades, infests, and infects every ongoing thought-process within the central nervous system.

I have hereby named this affliction "*Romantic Delusia*".

Romantic Delusia is the psychological realm a person operates from before experiencing, assimilating, and accepting the cold, hard Realities of Life.

It is quite a pleasant state of mind, which makes it difficult to distinguish from:

- A good mood
- Being in love
- A bloodstream full of potent narcotics.

It is from this state of mind where the Seeds of Hope flourish and take root.

It is where Dreams and Aspirations are Legally Permitted to Exist.

It is here, where, upon careful examination of What We Thought Life Was versus What It Really Is, opposing belief systems wage war within our conscious mind, creating an unbearable Cognitive Dissonance that *must* be resolved.

Once so, *Romantic Delusia* is converted from thought-form into miniscule, microscopic protein-bits, like pieces of film from a cutting-room floor, and passed out through the colon/urinary tracts.

Many of today's American Youth suffer from *Romantic Delusia*, symptoms including:

- Idealism
- Protest Movements
- Funny Hairstyles.

Many adults suffer further stages of this illusionary experience:

- They believe politicians, preachers, and businessmen who tell them "Everything's going to be O.K."
- They believe they are *invincible* while behind the wheel of a car, and that no harm can ever come to them, despite their disregard for traffic laws/discourtesy towards fellow roadsters.
- They believe each other when they exclaim, "I love you."

Many people & institutions either choose/employ careers that *deliberately* fuel and sustain *Romantic Delusia*:

- Self-Help Gurus
- Hollywood & Television
- Those who sell substances/chemicals, legally or illegally, designed to alter your state of consciousness.

If you ask me (although you don't need to, for it is imminent I am soon to offer forth another useless epiphany), the Only Occupation on this Planet that <u>does</u> <u>not</u> contribute in one form or another to Romantic Delusia is that of the *Funeral Parlor*.

—————————————————

For approximately thirty-nine years, I suffered from this very malady I would eventually come to name, and use as a chapter title in my first book, *Miscellaneous Hullabaloo*.

Many delusions took residence within my gray matter, and *paid no rent*.

When *Reality* often stopped by, unannounced and uninvited, it would often cause me extreme pain and discomfort (i.e., "*immaturity*"), and I would be forced to document these incidences on paper.

Sometimes, the Finished Product would prove uplifting, funny, and/or optimistic.

Other times, all it did was rhyme, rant, and regurgitate the Reality I Had Been Attempting To Keep At Bay. Most functioning, well-adjusted adults prefer to refer to such particular outbursts as *Denial*.

—————————————————

My first collection (which I haven't hesitated to mention *twice* already), *Miscellaneous Hullabaloo*, contained most of the positive, upbeat, and happy-go-lucky horseshit that usually accompanies *Romantic Delusia*.

This second collection, *Inane Balderdash*, includes All Those Intrusions that Reality Had Been Forcing Upon Me, Whether I Liked It Or Not.

So, if you have already experienced my first collection, *stand prepared*—this anthology will prove the *antithesis* of that Former Version of Myself who *Once Knew Hope*.

If not, that's quite all right. If opposites really do attract, then the other writings will eventually make their way to you somehow.

That's how the Universe *works*, you know.

Enjoy nonetheless!

Sincerely,

David Q. Tague
April Fools Day, 2009
Long Island, New York

INTRODUCTION

There were three distinct instances during my grade-school years that I remember getting in trouble.

One was a one-time offense. The second a kid can get arrested for now, and the third has become a Recurring Life Theme.

I don't know why I remembered these three at this precise time, but maybe it will lead us somewhere.

The "one-time offense" occurred in the first grade one morning when I went to sharpen a pencil before class started. Attempting to be the well-prepared student my teacher was brainwashing me to be, I assumed my actions to be timely/appropriate.

While grinding a wooden, lead-filled stick topped by a rubber tip within a canister screwed to the side of a wall, the "Pledge of Allegiance" began to boom over the school loudspeaker.

"I pledge of allegiance"—VRRUMM-VRRUMM-VRRUMM! "...to the flag"—WUMMA-WUMMA-WUMMA! "...of the United States of America..."—CLUNK.

"Go stand in the corner, young man! You don't sharpen your pencil during The Pledge!"

Had I known the *exact moment* whence the "P.O.A." was to commence, I would not have purposely disrupted its broadcast by going off to sharpen my pencil. Attempting to avoid the humiliation (and eventual discipline) of being "unprepared for class", why would I deliberately seek out unnecessary attention/trouble?

It was an honest mistake. I was *six years old*.

The second offense occurred that same year, and consisted of chasing the girls around the classroom and kissing them. Once again, I was only six years old. "Go stand in the corner!" *Again!*

This habit was a little more difficult to quit cold turkey, but I was catching on—school was not a place where one should 1) show affection, 2) make mistakes, or 3) act your age.

Got it!

———— ———— ———— ———— ———— ———— ———— ———— ———— ———— ———— ———— ———— ————

The third and final offense has now become a Recurring Theme in my life—as a seven year-old second grader, I often got in trouble for "laughing".

That's correct—*laughing*. I found a lot of thing's funny. I couldn't help it.

During film-strips or record-playing presentations, the teacher claimed that my laugh was too loud and disrupted the entire class. Guess where I ended up?"

Of course, these are fond memories of the years 1972-1974. I can add another, if you like—

I annoyed my second-grade teacher with my laughing so much, that, at the end of the year, she told everyone she was a *witch*, and that she was going to turn me into a *frog* the next morning, the last day of school!

I was *terrified*. I was only seven years old, and I *believed* her.

I shared these fears with my mother, who was not pleased with my teacher's behavior.

I believe, had she the proper opportunity, "Momma Q." would have done more to this "witch" than just make her *stand in the corner*.

———— ———— ———— ———— ———— ———— ———— ———— ———— ———— ———— ———— ———— ————

So, by the time I was eight years old, I was already guilty of:

- Treason
- Heterosexual Tendencies
- Having a Sense of Humor.

As one of my favorite cartoon characters of that time was wont to say: *"Dissssspicable!"*

———— ———— ———— ———— ———— ———— ———— ———— ———— ———— ———— ———— ———— ————

Of course, much has changed since 1974, such as clothing, hairstyles, and technology.

I am not sure *I have changed much* since 1974, other than becoming taller.

Nowadays, in 2007, Having a Sense of Humor is bound to offend at least 50% of the American Population. It's gotten so bad we've had to banish (segregate) those who happen to be funny onto their own cable TV channel (Comedy Central), and even this is no guarantee against future retribution/retaliation from many whom have willfully placed themselves in direct opposition to personality traits such as:

a) clever wit,
b) happiness, &
c) frequent laughter.

Nowadays, in 2007, being attracted to the opposite sex may or may not contain the potential to offend:

- Gays and Lesbians
- Heterosexuals Themselves, whose favorite past-times may or may not include:
  1. Wife-Beating
  2. Men-Bashing
  3. Infidelity
  4. Rape
  5. Battling for Head of Household Status
  6. Divorce
  7. Sexual Harassment Lawsuits.

Nowadays, in 2007, unless you have your own network news platform where you can sit behind a desk for an hour, holding a pen you'll never write with, and spend the entire time criticizing Other

Fellow Americans, you can pretty much consider yourself a *Traitor*—you're bound to disagree with one of these "geniuses" eventually, and when you do, this is what they will prefer to refer to you as. Remember, without <u>Enemies</u>, *There Is No Show.*

What does it all *mean*?

Absolutely <u>*nothing*</u>—its all *Inane Balderdash,* documented here by Yours Truly, in another feeble, yet time-wasting attempt to be "prepared for class".

For these appear to be the Only Valuable Skills I have acquired from my Early Years of Grammar-School Persecution:

- Placing letters of the alphabet in sequences that form words
- Placing words in sequences that form sentences
- Placing sentences in sequences that form paragraphs.

Thank the Universe hence, as I got taller, I developed enough initiative, drive, and desire to eventually master the following, yet somewhat-related skills:

- Placing titles above these paragraphs once they formed a complete concept/theme
- Gathering enough themes to add up to at least 150-or-so printed pages
- Successfully placing these 150-plus pages between two covers under a Main Title
- Publishing, promoting, and selling these ideas to *you*, either to:
  a) Remind you of, or
  b) Distract you from
     1. The fact that we are all going to *die.*

In other words, *That's Entertainment!*

Last
Things
First

Look What I See!

Hey, Gang!

Today is Tuesday, November 13, 2007
And I am beginning to compile
The Necessary Works
For my 'Second Collection of Mayhem'!

It's five o'clock in the morning
And I'm boilin' water for coffee
And smokin' cigarettes
Out in my truck
('cause it's raining outside)

I'm on vacation
But instead of travelin'
(like I had the money
or the will to do so)
I'm-a-*writin'!*

It always happens like this—

You Start One Project
And an Idea Invades Your Sphere of Awareness
So Instead of Getting Done
What You Originally Intended To Do
You Follow the Muse
You Write It Down
And Add It To The Pile...

Let's get on with it, shall we?

The name of this poem

Is "Look What I See!"

So permit me to allow myself

To begin…

Look What I See!

I see situations
that refuse to solve problems
I see lots of people
Who Like It That Way
I see set-ups and circuses
Folks who make purchases
Based on Emotion
(Not Logic or Budget)
I see businesses, governments
Organizations—
Agencies, synagogues
Churches and cults
Shopping malls, traffic jams
Holiday Madness!
(it all cools down
once the new year begins)
I see competition
And elimination—
Downsizing/upgrading
Makeovers, *murders!*
Jealousy, Apathy,
Therapy, *Rage!*
Uncontrolled Tempers
That Make the Front Page
I see families struggling
Two parents juggling

Two careers each
Just to eat and pay taxes
I see women with implants
And guys with hair-weaves
Everyone's on a cell-phone
Everyone except *me*...

— — — — — — — — — — — — — —

I've got more to say
About all that I see
So just keep turnin' pages
And join in the fun!

I wrote this piece last
But I'm putting it *first*
Because It Introduces
The Rest Of The Show

Quite nicely, I think!
(then again, it's *me* talking—
I *wrote* it, of course—
Now It's My Job To Sell It)

So press ahead, Onward!
Come Share What I See
A Diversion For You
And for me—

"*Royalties!*"

   (...might as well be honest right from the get-go, yes/no?)

Parking Lot Poet

<u>Chorus</u> (open with…)

I'm a Parking Lot Poet
That's my occupation
I've done other work
Attempted many vocations

But a paper and pen
Is what seems to suit me
A Parking Lot Poet's
All I'll Ever Be

Take a minute to listen
Cause I've been around awhile
I promise not to waste your time
Or cramp your style

I'm probably gonna tell you
What you already know
At least comin' out to see me
Gave you somewhere to go

I'm gonna talk all about
Peace, war, love & hate
All the topics that we like to
Sit around and debate

Maybe politics/religion
Just to stir up the pot
Or remind you of the many things
We still haven't got

(CHORUS)

Now I've looked and I've listened
For many odd-years
I've studied just what makes us laugh
And brings on the tears

I've pondered what the hell
We're doing here on this earth
What it is I could accomplish
That would have any worth

I watched fellow humans
As they suffered and toiled
Some had a good attitude
Some folks were just spoiled

I've seen people doing good
And never get a reward
I've seen people doing nothin'
And complain they were bored

(CHORUS)

Now let's take a minute
Turn attention on me
You knew I'd talk about myself
Eventually

I've got a big ego
I'm an artist, remember?
I'm a Cancer
I was born in July, Not December

That last rhyme was cheap
But it's the best I could do
Sometimes I have to make up words
Like "Hap Bidda Boo"

Just to make the verses flow
And to convey what I mean
To explain to you in rhymes
All that I've lived, done and seen

(CHORUS)

So I see you all waiting
For my next revelation
What it is that I can say
To bring about your salvation

Will I answer all your questions
Or just raise a few more
You'll have to stay the whole performance
To know just what's in store

Cause I've got a slew of tunes
And boy, are you folks in luck
I wrote 'em all in parking lots
While sittin' in my truck

Now I've got the opportunity
To share them with you
Allow me to introduce myself—
My name's David Q.!

(and, How Do You Do?)

Everybody's Famous (...It's Official!) [18 September 2007]

I have documented this
For Posterity
(including the date at the top of this page)

Just in case there's a World War
Or a Holocaust
And Everything Gets Destroyed
(Except a copy of this book, *Inane Balderdash*)

and some sole survivor finds it
(hopefully he/she can read English)
and wonders,
"...what was Life Like Before All This Happened?"

Well, lemme tell ya all about it

Here goes, listen up, Pilgrim—

At the time, I,

David Q. Tague

Wrote this poem (I am actually writing it now)

It became apparent to all Three Of Us

(Me, Myself and I)

while home watching television (exercise)

for the past few days

and nursing bronchitis

that

Everybody's Famous!

That's right, gang! *Everyone!*

Everyone On The Planet Earth was Famous Back in 2007—

- if you got lost on a camping trip, you became famous
- if you ran out on your soon to be wife/husband, you became famous
- if you filmed yourself going to the bathroom and put it on the internet, you became famous
- if you won as a contestant on a reality T.V. show, you became famous
- if you LOST as a contestant on a reality T.V. show, you became famous
- if you suffered some unfortunate disaster, like being trapped down in a coal mine or had your life support pulled, you became famous
- if you woke up, got out of bed, went to work, and came home, you had a good shot at becoming famous, because sometime during the course of your day, you were probably being filmed.

Back in My Time (2007), it became so easy to become famous that it wasn't a Big Deal anymore! Everyone just assumed that Everybody Else was Famous!

Everybody had his or her own talk show. Everybody wrote a book! Everyone had an Album/CD out! Everybody got promoted at his or her jobs! Everybody Made Millions of Dollars!

Everybody was *Special...*

So, *you*, as a sole survivor of an Earthly Misfortune are asking yourself (in English, I hope), "What the hell happened to Everybody?"

Did Global Warming flood the planet?

Did a Nuclear Missile kill all but a few?

Disease? Plague? Meteor shower?

As they used to say in things called "tests", *'none of the above.'*

Here's what happened—
Everybody Became So Famous
And So Important
And So Special
That They Became Like Gods
And You Couldn't Tell Them Anything
Without Them Offending Each Other
Because Everybody Knew Everything
—Hell, they were *Famous!*



They Had The Information

And The Skills

And the Knowlegde

And The Power

And The Influence

To Refashion The Universe (makeover)

To Conform It To Their Own Image

Which was Great and Wonderful,

Except…

…no one could agree on anything!

Everyone's Vision Was Different—

- How To Save The World

- How To Fix The Environment

- How To Create Wealth

- How To Run your Business

- How to Look and Feel 20 Years Younger (even if you're only 19!)

- How To Deal With Difficult People

- How To Lose Weight

- How To Build Muscle and Burn Fat

- How to Cure Disease

- How To Worship God

- How To Rid Ourselves of Religion

- How To Have A Bigger Erection

- How We Should Promote Abstinence

- How To Keep Our Kids Off Drugs

- How We Should Be Tolerant of All People

- How Zero Tolerance Will Reduce Violence In The Workplace…

How…How… and *HOW!*

Everybody was Famous

And Everyone Was Special

Whether they Won or Lost

Lived or Died

Killed or Saved

Broiled or Fried

And You Couldn't Tell Anybody *Anything…*

▬ ▬ ▬ ▬ ▬ ▬ ▬ ▬ ▬ ▬ ▬ ▬ ▬ ▬

So, we started

Firing People From Their Jobs

And Running Each Other Off the Road

And Refusing To Help Each Other Out

Assuming and assigning these types of "Shit Details"

To Some "Imaginary Agency"

So We Wouldn't Have To Take Blame

For The Problems We Ourselves Were Causing

All The While

Spouting About It

On Our Own Talk Shows

And In TV Specials

And In Our Movies and Music

And In Our Books

(such as this one)

And we blamed each other

And we neglected each other

Till We Eventually

Killed Ourselves Off

Waiting for the

Imaginary Agency

To Save Us…

Of course, All Of This Didn't Happen YET—

For I am still writing this poem

And am Still Alive

On 09/18/2007 9:59:22 AM

But I Am Warning Everyone Now

Because We Are At The Beginning of this Vision

And We Don't See It Coming Because

We're

     All

        Too

           Busy

              Being

                 Famous…

They Did It For Me

When Chuck Jones Drew
And Mel Blanc Voiced
All Those Cartoons
They Broadcast To Me
On My TV
I Was Too Young To Realize
They Did It For Me…

When Don Adams yelled "Chumley!"
Or, "Sorry about that, Chief!"
Made a call on his shoe-phone
(thanks to Mel Brooks and Buck Henry)
I was too busy laughing to see
That They Did It All For Me

When Monty Python
Went in search for The Grail
And the Meaning of Life
Imitating horses with coconuts
Bearing tidings of lupines
Performing "silly-walks"
And blowing up people behind bushes
Skits segueing into cartoons
Not afraid of being buffoons
That in sacrificing their sanity
They Did It All For Me.

   — — — — — — — — — — — — — — — —

The Beatles made All Those Albums
Just For Me
So did The Eagles and ELP
(and CCR/John Fogerty)
Lest we forget Stan Lee

Who drew Spiderman Just For Me?
Or The Electric Company?
Or ABC, CBS & NBC?
Donny and Marie?
Lee Majors did The Six Million Dollar Man
Just For Me
Evil Knievel jumped the Grand Canyon
Just For Me
Adam West starred in Batman
Just For Me
(Don't leave out Superman/George Reeves/Christopher Reeve!)

Clint Eastwood said, "Make My Day"
And starred in "Every Which Way"
And his movies made a Sudden Impact
In many people's lives
Whether he worked with Don Siegel
Or Sergio Leone
He Did It All Just For Me…

In 1969, the Mets won
The World Series
In 1977, then,
The Yankees
1979 onward
Islanders Stanley Cups
Jack LaLanne
Doin' 1000 Push-Ups!

Inventions, New Movements
And Philosophies
Diets, Health Food Stores
And Fitness Machines
The Army, the Navy,
The Air Force, *Marines*…

They're All Doin' It
Just For Me!

How about Martin Mull
Jerry Seinfeld, George Carlin?
Bill Cosby/Fat Albert
Elvis, Dean Martin, & 'Marlon'?

Henry, Pete, Jane and Bridget
Jimmy Stewart, "The Duke"—
Fred Gwynne & John Astin
(who once married Patty Duke!)

Major Nelson and Jeannie
Darren Stevens and Sam
The Banana Splits, Monkees
The Archies, Oh, *Man!*

If I sit here long enough
I'll re-live my Whole Life
So I'll stop here for now
So as not to exhaust you

There's much more to cover
In between these bound pages
So I'll stop here for now
(I think you get the point)

I can always come back to this
(write a "Part Two")
But for now, Let's Get On
With The Rest Of The Show

For, As All The Fore-Mentioned
Have Brought Me Much Joy
It Is Now My Turn
To Attempt Something Similar

Just For You.

The Answer

If you waitin' for things to get better
You might be waitin' a long, long time
If you savin', and 401-K'n
Da market crash when your cash in it's prime

You buy a new car, and somebody dent it
You can't afford no house, so you rent it
Another crack in da pavement, cement it
You can't open da gate, somebody bent it

Here come disaster, its peekin' round da corner
Don't lift da covers or da monsters will come
Whatever you do, don't ever take no risk now
Just stands still, and plays like you dumb!

If you thinkin', somebody gonna "fix it"
You must be dreamin', cause they already tried
Every time a good man spoke their good mind
They ate bullets for breakfast, and the people cried...

{You can protest, and you can fight
You can stay up and complain all night!
Da world's da same as it's Always Gonna Be
So here's a lesson for you, in Futility!}

Who knows, when this Whole Thing Started
Well, we can contemplate, ponder and guess
We've tried to make it work here for centuries
No matter what we do it end up a mess

It just a Rerun, This Whole Existence
Predict da Future just by Watchin' da Past
So start laughin' now, cause you never know
Just how long our short lives are gonna last...

19

Trolls,
Dwarfs,
&
Leprechauns

October 15, 2006

To: Trollastic Books, Inc.
123 Lollipop Circle
Suite 3 ½ (Feet Tall!)
Canasta, New York 6789Ten

Dearest Sirs & Madams;

Included herein is the "final draft" manuscript of "Trolls, Dwarfs, & Leprechauns", for submission to your Editorial Staff, concerning said corrections applicable to the Plot Structure of our First Children's Book.

Confident that this story is bound to capture & illuminate the hearts and minds of millions of American children, we have already completed three chapters for a "second installment", and have brainstormed a list of future titles for a possible "series". If interest behooves, we will be more than happy to e-mail/fax them over, at our convenience.

Thank you once again for helping us get into print. We look forward to our upcoming business meeting on the 32nd.

Sincerely,

Dr. D. Sherbert and J. Lloyd, Esq.

Once upon a time, there was a Troll who lived in the sumps of Bethpage.

His name was Fred Small, and he used to work at the bowling alley.

One day, he observed a horror that he *could not bear.*

While setting up the pins one Friday Evening, a group of Normal-Sized People came in to bowl.

Joining them were some Midgets and Dwarfs.

"What's *this*?" he said to himself. "*Little People* usually do not mingle with *Assholes!*"

Fred often referred to Normal Sized People as *Assholes*, based on The Manner In Which They Behaved Towards "Little People" such as himself.

For example, while having his supper in the sumps on a Saturday Evening, he overheard a loud & obnoxious "Group of Assholes" talking about the Little People through their kitchen window.

"What's the difference between *midgets* and *dwarfs*?" inquired one.

"I dunno, but they're hiring them more frequently at the supermarket!" barked another Asshole.

"I think we have a Troll squatting in the sump!" claimed yet a third.

"*There goes the neighborhood!*" all three laughed in unison, finishing their marijuana.

At the bowling alley, Fred would re-set the pins that the machines did not lift properly.

It was difficult for Normal-Sized People to work in such confined spaces, and for such little wages.

Mr. Gemmelsteen, Fred's Boss, always hired Little People to Do the Jobs that *Most American's Didn't Want to Do.*

This particular Friday, Fred was working a double-shift, due to many sick-calls.

The pin machines were working well, but poor Fred was tired.

Then, it *happened.*

The Normal Sized People and the Midgets and Dwarfs took up residence on Lane Seven to begin bowling.

Fred was at the Snack Bar on his 3-Minute Break, eating a pretzel.

He noticed that no one had brought any bowling balls with them, nor sought out any provided by the alley.

The Normal Sized People began to pick up the Little People and throw them down the bowling lane!

"SMASH!" went the pins!

"Strike!" one of the Assholes hollered.

Fred froze in place and stared in amazement—shocked, stunned, & appalled.

"Break's over, Small!" shouted Mr. Gemmelsteen. "Back to work!"

"Are you responsible for this?" Fred asked the boss.

"What are you talking about?" asked Mr. Gemmelsteen.

"Throwing Little People Down the Alley? Do you think this is *funny*?"

"I run a business, Small. If I don't bring in customers, you don't get your $6.75 an hour!"

"Stick it up your asshole, *Asshole*!" hollered Fred. "I QUIT!"

Fred hired the law firm of "Acapella and Krishna" to handle his Discrimination Case.

"Little People Have *Rights*!" he demanded.

Small vs. Gemmelsteen went to court, and awarded Fred with a Large Settlement.

However, it would take him quite some time to receive his money.

During this interim, Fred could not find employment, due to the popularity of his case, which was all over the news.

Employers were too scared to hire Fred Small, because they were afraid he would try to take away *their money* too!

Fred would call the Law Firm every day and ask, "Is my money here yet?"

"These things take time," said his Counsel, N.S. Crowe. "I'll call you as soon as we get a check!"

"*Friggin' Normal-Sized People!*" grumbled Fred Small.

Days, weeks, and months went by, and Fred Small could no longer pay his bills.

He was eventually evicted from his basement apartment in Plainedge, and took to drinking beer and smoking cigarettes in order to cope.

Having nowhere to live, he found new residence in the Bethpage Sumps.

"What is taking me so long to get my money?" wondered Fred Small, as he stood, wobbling and balancing himself against the large plate-glass window outside *Kweenie's Korner*, peering in at the "Lottoball TV Set", hoping to strike it rich.

After losing another five dollars, he proceeded indoors to read some porno and eat some gray ham and brown bologna.

He washed it down with a bottle of cranberry juice containing an expiration date that of two years prior, but he didn't care.

"I'm going to get my money!" he sputtered, tripping over a cigar stub left on the floor by one of the regulars.

With the last couple of dollars to his name, Fred Small hopped a bus out to Acapella and Krishna in Port Franklin.

Intoxicated and reeking of cold cuts, he proceeded past the front desk without an appointment and up to the office of N.S. Crowe.

When he arrived, he noticed a different nameplate on the door.

Samuel Stretch was the new lawyer now occupying Mr. Crowe's former office.

"What is going on? Where is Mr. Crowe? Let me in!" hollered Fred, banging on the door.

Two Security Guards materialized immediately and pried Fred away. Kicking and screaming as he was tossed out onto the hard pavement like a sack of garbage, Fred hollered, "It's a *conspiracy!* It's the *government!*"

Part of what he said was *true*.

There *was* a conspiracy behind Fred not receiving his settlement.

But it had nothing to do with the *government*.

It had *everything* to do with *Samuel Stretch*.

Samuel Stretch took over Fred's case shortly after N.S. Crowe accepted a higher-paying/more condescending position with another law firm.

Samuel Stretch received Fred's settlement money shortly thereafter, but did not contact him.

Samuel Stretch had *issues* with the Little People.

When Samuel was seven years old, he saw the "Wizard of Oz" for the first time on television.

He enjoyed every part until it came to the "Munchkins".

These "Little People" gave him *nightmares.*

As Samuel got older, he grew, grew & *grew!*

By the time he entered the sixth grade, he was almost *six feet tall!*

Everyone was little compared to him, and he felt like an *outcast.*

Being taller than the average person was painful enough. But seeing these "Little People" just made him feel worse, and he avoided them at every turn.

"Am I a freak, just like them?" he would often inquire of himself during unpleasant internal dialogue.

Now, he had to *help* one of them.

Samuel Stretch had a *phobia* concerning the Little People.

A Phobia is an Irrational Fear that invades a person's thought processes and prevents them from leading normal, happy, & productive lives.

Samuel Stretch had a fear that one day, the Little People would kidnap him and make him work in a *bakery* against his will.

Fred Small was now desperate for cash.

He no longer had money for cigarettes, beer, or Lottoball.

What was he to do?

It was now the month of October, and Fred froze his buns off in the sump, waiting for teenagers to throw beer bottles and fast-food scraps over the fence.

He overheard them talking this particular Saturday evening: "You guys going to the Halloween Dance?"

Just then, Fred Small got an *idea*...

He quickly finished some stale french fries and moseyed uptown to the St. Vincent de Paul's Clothing Drop Box.

He rummaged through all the green material he could find, cutting and weaving with his Swiss Army Knife.

Within three hours, Fred Small had a "Leprechaun Costume"!

Halloween arrived, and Fred Small went "Trick-or-Treating" in Port Franklin.

He headed to the Law Offices of Acapella and Krishna.

He followed behind a group of little children and their parents who were hitting up the business district for all the free candy they could get.

Fred made it past the security guards and into the elevator.

The double-doors parted with a "*whoosh!*" and he made his way to Samuel Stretch's Office.

The door was open, and Samuel was on the phone.

"Trick or treat, you Greedy Gargantuan!" hollered Fred Small, jumping over Samuel's desk.

Samuel, terrified, dropped the receiver and tried to escape.

Fred kicked him in the ankle, and all seven feet of him collapsed like a tree "timbering" down in the forest!

"Where's my money, you giant bastard!" screamed Fred, pinning Samuel by his neck.

"It's---it's---"

In a rage, Fred pulled an old guitar pick out of his pocket, and rammed it halfway up Samuel's left nostril. *"Answer me!"*

Just before pissing his pants and passing out, Samuel Stretch warbled, "Middle…left…desk…drawer——please…no… more… meringue…pies…"

A beefy, thick-necked Nassau County Corrections Officer approached Fred Small's jail cell.

"You're free to go", he muttered, unlocking the steel doors.

"Who posted bail?" asked Fred, without a friend in the world.

"The guy you brutalized. He's not filing any charges."

Fred Small walked out of the precinct and hailed a cab.

— — — — — — — — — — — — — — —

It was about 11 months later, and Frederick Small admired the shine from his bowling shoes as he observed the happy patrons at the "Leprechaun Bowling Alley".

He bought out Gemmelsteen, who went bankrupt shortly after discontinuing "Midget Bowling Night". Fred was now the proud, new owner of his very-own establishment.

Fred gulped down the remainder of his "Stretch-Size" Jumbo Beer available at his "Munchkin Snack Bar", and watched in amusement as seven dwarfs threw a "Normal-Sized Person" down the alley for a 10th-Frame, 7-10 Split Spare.

"*Assholes!*" he laughed, summoning Gemmelsteen for another "Jumbo".

THE END.

Epics

The Artist

The Artist
Is not someone
You are going to
Fully understand

You may
Admire their works
But their lifestyle
Will baffle you

They see the world
Much differently
Than most folks

And rarely,
(if ever)
fit into the "system"

The artist
Became an artist
Because Life Prepared
Him/Her for it

Life gave them
Different sets
Of circumstances

Than the rest
Of the folks
In the "system"

Or, maybe
Denied them the pleasures/luxuries
That the "system"
Freely offered the rest

Causing the
"artist-in-training"
to obsess

and
ask,
"Why?"

—————————————————————

The Artist

Is an Outsider

An Observer

An Historian

An Innovator

They are not
Part of the "machine"

Rather, they
"create"
New Machines

And the "system'
Does it's best
To reject them
And point out—
"Observe the fool
and his folly!"

———————————————

But
Sometimes
Accidents
Happen

And for
Some strange
Reason .

People
'take'
to the Artist

and a
"following"
ensues

and people say
"Look at the artist!"

and then they say,
"Genius!"

———————————————

But it's a
Long, Hard Road

And the Only Way
that the Artist
Can fit
Into the "system"
Is to
"not fit"

because they
see the
horse-shit
that goes on

and refuse
to take part
in perpetuating

all the tricks
and traumas

that are
deliberately
designed

to keep
everyone else

from
becoming
an
"artist"…

The Artist
Takes time out
To observe
The beauty
That Life
Has to offer

Of Nature
And its
Grand Design

While the
Rest of the World
Is busy
Keeping the "system" going

Mastering cliches
Such as
"Same shit,
different day"

and
"Life's a bitch
and then you die"

and the best
bumper-sticker
of them all:

"he who
dies with
the most
toys wins…"

*Wins "**what**"?*
The artist asks…

But the
Rest of the World
Doesn't ask

They just want
To "win"

They can't bear
The humiliation
Of "losing"

Even if
They have
No Idea
What It Is
That They
Are Supposed
To Be
Winning
Or
Losing…

The Artist
Knows the
"Ultimate Truth"

He/She
Knows that
Everybody Loses
In this Life

And that
When folks
"Think"
they
are "winning"

Life
Is Only
Setting
Them
Up
For
The
Kill…

—————————————————

The Artist
Learns this
Early on

Most folks
Don't catch on
Until it's
Too Late

And some
Never arrive
At this conclusion at all
(and are probably
better off for it)

But, in
Any event

(as an
uncle of mine
is wont
to exclaim
at the beginning
of any sentence)

The Artist
Does
His/Her
Best

To
Absorb
Life
Like a sponge

And
Get the most and the best
That they can

Out of
A
"Universally-Imposed
Time-Limit"

And attempt
To the
Best of their
Ability and potential

To share
Their discoveries
With others

Imposing on
Their free time
And busy schedules

Just to say,

"LOOK!"

"LISTEN!"

"THINK!"

"FEEL!"

"TASTE!"

"TOUCH!"

"TRY!"

⸺⸺⸺⸺⸺⸺⸺⸺⸺⸺⸺⸺⸺⸺

You may never
Understand
The Artist

But
He/She
Understands you

Better than
You'll ever know

And sometimes
They may appear
Totally insane

43

And sometimes
You may not care
For what they have to say

And sometimes
They may
Overstep their bounds

Thinking
Who
They
Are

So
Full
Of
Themselves

That they
Refuse
To let
The
Rest of the World
In
On
Their
"little jokes"

and then,
have the nerve
to look down
their noses
at you
for not
"getting" it...

Sometimes,
The Artist
Is a
Pompous Ass

And some folks
"mistake"
themselves
for
Artists

When
Logic
And
Reason
Clearly
Dictate

That
They are
Only Desperate Souls
Seeking Love and Attention
They Never Received

At Some
Earlier Point In Time

So, they have to
"perform"
in order to "get"
What Everyone Else "Got"
Free of Charge…

It is not easy
To live
With an Artist

Because they keep Odd Hours

And think about things
That most people
Wouldn't bother to put
Into their brains

And they can wear on you

Because they
Don't want to do the same things
That everyone else does

And they don't
Say the same things
That everyone else does

And so,
They disrupt your plans
And they disrupt your life

And while
The Artist
Simultaneously
Pleases the Fans,
They cause you
Nothing but grief…

Do not try
To understand
The Artist

Most of the time,
They
Don't even
Understand themselves

They "have" to "create"

They cannot help it

They have to
Stop what they are doing
At any given moment

And Start their Art

Before the Inspiration Vanishes

Before it Dies…

An Artist
May not make for

The Best Employee

Or the Best Friend

Or the Best Lover

Or the Best Person

You Have Ever Known

Because their Passion

Is Their Art

Which is their Work

Which is their Life

And these three are inseparable

And cannot be scheduled

Like a 40-hour workweek

Or a holiday barbecue

Or a road trip…

—————————————————————

The Artist's "Authority"

Is "Inspiration"

And they must follow it

Till they exhaust it

And this angers the folks

Closest to them

But when

The Finished Product is Complete

And On Display

The Artist

Is Loved Once Again

If Only from Afar…

————————————————

The Artist
Is a Hero
To his/her fans

And an
Annoyance
To those
That must
Deal with
He/she

This is
The way
It must
Always be

And the
Only Thing
Other than
Death and Taxes
(cliché?)
that will

probably

never

change

———————————————————

(<u>P.S.</u>: it is impossible to "love" an artist. Just enjoy the "art"—you'll
suffer fewer headaches.)

swerve

as I was heading home from 7-11
early this morning (5:10AM)
a funny thing happened to me
while driving

there was nobody else on the road
besides me and an
oncoming car
in the opposing lane

there was a plastic
garbage can lid
resting in the lane
of the opposing driver

of course
we had to cross paths
just as we both passed this
object in the road

and instead of
hitting the brakes

the Other Driver
swerved as to
Not Hit The
Garbage Can Lid

Almost Crashing
Directly Into Me.

if you were to ask me
the Basis for
My Sense of Humor

I would tell you
That what I find
Most amusing

Is when
People have
The Clear, Correct, and
Obvious Opportunity
For Doing The
Thing That
Makes The Most Sense

But instead,
They choose the
Course of Action
That is
Guaranteed
To Bring About
The Most
Undesired
Of Results.

It seems that folks
Nowadays
Care more about
Garbage Can Lids
Than they do about
Other People

They put
"Save the Animals"
Bumper Stickers
On their cars

And proceed to
Kill each other
Over
Parking Spaces

They screw each other
In business deals
And wonder,
"What's wrong with
the Economy?"

They have
(somewhere along the line)
replaced
"please" and "thank you"
with
running you off the road
in the mad dash to work
and cutting in front of you
on line at the store

all the while,
commercials
for new medications
fill my television screen
3 times an hour,
purportedly

curing one ailment,
yet offering
(free of charge)
four
additional
illness
symptoms…

My neighbors are too tired
To wave to me
From across the street
(Even though they can see me)

But they are never too tired
To order products
Off of a computer
Or from an infomercial

And, in those
Rare occasions that we accidentally
Bump into each other
And force pleasant conversation

They are never too tired
To tell me
what a great deal
They got on their
New car or
Some furniture or
Some other
Useless possession
Or just 'parrot' (verb)
What I already heard
In the news
And read
In the papers…

Somewhere along the line,
Everyone in this country became
An Expert
And a Bad-Ass

Everybody Knows Everything
And if you prove them wrong,
They'll kick your teeth in

They wear their hats backwards
And shirts that say "No Fear"

They park in fire lanes
And handicapped spots
When their legs work
Perfectly well

And they All Believe that they
"Entitled" to something,
and assume that there is some
Imaginary Agency (in existence)
Willing and Waiting
To Grant Their Wishes
At Any Given Time...

Be it money,
Respect,
Or .03 cents off a can of string beans
At the supermarket
Without a coupon

Something is Wanted
Before Something is Offered

And If We Don't Get Our Way
We Have The Right
To Remain Nasty

And Anything That We Say
Won't Be Used Against Us

Because The Customer is
Always Right
And Has The Right
To Behave Like A
Selfish Spoiled-Rotten Toddler
In Order To
Prove Their Point.

_____

It's a shame
That we're not taught
Wisdom instead of
<u>History</u>

And *Manners*
Instead of
<u>Religion</u>

Because we haven't learned anything from either

Oh, I forgot—We Already *Know Everything!*

_____

That being the case,
Who is it that
chooses to risk
A car accident

In order to miss
Running over
A plastic
Garbage can lid?

Everyone's So Tough
But they ain't running to the
Recruiter
To Sign Up

And Everyone Knows Everything
But they're not
Running for Office

Maybe I should
Take My Own Advice
And teach
Driver's Ed?

1994 again

I wish
It was
1994
again

when I was
28
and not
41

I had
More
Energy
Back then

And
Believed
More
Lies…

Back in 1994, a two-bedroom apartment
Went for $600.00 a month
And you could still
Eat quite well
Without having to worry

Now, it is 2007
And
You are LUCKY
If you can get
A studio apartment
For
$1000.00...

· · · · · · · · · · · · · · ·

1994
was the last time
I had been
On an airplane

Now,
In 2007,
I hate just having
To get into my car

To have to go
To a crowded supermarket
Full of screaming kids
And angry adults

Back in 1994
You could go to a store
And actually have
A good time with your chore...

· · · · · · · · · · · · · · ·

Back in 1994
You could still play a guitar
And people
Would listen

Now,
In 2007
You don't have to
Play an instrument to be heard

You can become
Instantly Famous
If you sing
Other people's songs

On a
Reality TV Show
And everyone will love you
Even if you lose…

In 2007
Everyone else
Is
Believing the lies

That I
Left behind
In
1994

They are
Having
All
The fun

While
Half my life
Is
Over and Done...

I must appear
As a fire-breathing dragon
To the birds
Outside on the feeder

As I smoke cigarettes
And watch them eat
In between verses
Of writing this lament

I never watched birds
In 1994
Or cared
Much for animals back then

I'm allergic
To cats and dogs
And lately
My tolerance for humans is...

In 1994
I used to be tough
Now I'm just a
Powder-puff

In 1994
I was a stud
In 2007
I'm just a dud

I'm still too young
To be feeling so old
But now, my trade
Is poems told

Back then,
This would have been a song
But now,
I see where I went wrong…

I rhymed
Much more
In
'94

it's not
a
talent
anymore

these days,
it's an
annoyance—
bore

provoking
more yawns
than
ever before…

pretty soon,
computers
and
robots

will be doing
all
the
jobs

That
Americans
No
Longer

Wish
To
Do

and
pretty soon,
evolution
will

shrink
our
brains,
and

we
will
be
right

63

back
where
we
started…

—————————————————

all that will be
required
of the
human race

is to
sit around
and
be served

while
machinery
and
technology

do
all
the
work

—————————————————

I am
Thankful
That
The

Computer
Replaced
The
Typewriter

But I'm
Not
So
Sure

About
Anything
Else
Anymore…

———————————————————————

you see,
the
computer
also

replaced
common sense
and
reality to a degree

you can
see what
I mean

When
You watch a car commercial and
The vehicle switches terrain's twenty-five times
(thanks to C.G.I.)
Without ever having to leave the road…

———————————————————————

people believe what they are told
and if they are not given
what they were promised
they will get upset

so when they purchase the car
that switched terrain's twenty-five times on TV
yet can barely get through one terrain
in real life
without stalling

the customer is going to be angry
and blame another person
for lying
to them

all
because
of
a computer trick…

———————————————————————

as
has
been stated
previously

66

everyone else
is
now
believing

the
lies
that
I

Left
Behind
In
1994

so
once
again,
my

belief system
does not
match
up

with
that
of
my peers

and
I
Am
Forced

To
Sit
Behind
a
computer screen
and complain
about how
things were so much better in the past

when
you and I
both
know

that it's
all
a
load of horse-shit

and thirteen years from now
in 2020
I'll be somewhere
Writing about

How much better
Things were
Back in
2007…

Ain't Life Grand?

⸺ ⸺ ⸺ ⸺ ⸺ ⸺ ⸺ ⸺ ⸺ ⸺ ⸺ ⸺ ⸺ ⸺

(…now, I have to wait about ten days for this poem to *ferment*, then,
come back to it, look it over, feel proud of myself and how astute/

brilliant/perceptive I am, and go off to write it's *total antithesis* at a date
somewhat later than the moments in which I am currently stuck.)

{Disclaimer: There is no sound, logical evidence on record to prove
that 1994, was, in fact, a Better Year than 2007.}

[Note: Four out of five humans surveyed recommended "dumb" for
their *patience*, which *grew* dumb.]

"Consumerica"

You Wanna Give Me Your Money

C'mon! Hand it over—
I know you got some!
Just $15.95
Is all I'm asking

C'mon! Fork it up—
It ain't like you broke!
Anything under twenty bucks
These days, is a *bargain!*

Aw, come on, man—
What else you gonna do?
Rent a lame DVD
Or pay off a parking ticket?

C'mon, let's get to it!
Don't try to deny it—
Today is payday and
You Wanna Give Me Your Money!

C'mon, people!
I know you can afford it—
Home renovations and
Fancy new clothes

C'mon, folks, get with it!
Your gas tanks are full
The kids are all fed
Now it's time for a purchase!

C'mon, what's the holdup?
Just pull out your billfold!
Fish through that pocketbook
Or get to the bank

C'mon, let's get to it!
Uncle "ATM's" waiting—
My book's out and
You Wanna Give Me Your Money!

When Did It Change?

Remember back, when people had talent?
They used to hit home runs without any drugs
We used to follow examples, have heroes
Now we just worship criminals and thugs

We're cheating ourselves
And we're too dumb to know it
Of this we're proud
And not afraid to show it   (DUH!)

Remember back, when people had manners?
We used to say things like "thank you" and "please"
Now when we roll up to the fast food drive-thru
We holler, "Gimme two whoppers wit' cheese!"

We've got no class
No decency, no culture
We fed our Common Sense
Right to the vultures!   (CHOMP!)

We're getting' fat, when we should be healthy
We're goin' broke despite our 401-K
Technology increased productivity
Now we're doin' twice the work for half of the pay

I'm no moralist and I ain't perfect
Maybe I'm makin' all this up 'cause I'm nuts
I just miss the World I Used To Live In

(Way Back Before
it was considered "attractive"
to belong to
big, fat "butts"!)

When did it change?

The Rain Won't Keep 'Em Away

The rain won't keep 'em away
They just keep on arriving
Anxious to purchase and to consume
Everything they're advertising

The "Box" tells them what to get
Soon they start up their cars and they're driving
Ready to kill you for a parking space
And some wheeling, dealing, conniving!

Chorus

What is happening to you and me?
When did we all become so greedy?
What are we afraid we'll run out of?
In this bountiful 'Land of Plenty'?

The rain won't keep 'em away
Still they keep on complaining
That Everything is Overpriced or Out of Stock
Yet, they don't complain that it's raining?

Their minds won't let them forget
All the Bargains in the Flyer
Or every Holiday Sale on the Radio
"Yes, we need a New Deep Fat Fryer"!

Chorus II

What has happened to Society?
How did we all become so nasty?
If we don't lighten up and unwind---
Might as well wave 'Goodbye' to this country!

<u>Bridge</u>

Whatever you do---
Don't say "please" or "thank you"
Just bark out an item
And expect us to "fetch" it   (8 beats dead music/drum thump)

Always, remember to---
Talk down to the cashier or the
Clerk that's assisting you!

(Retail Solo!)

The rain won't keep 'em away
'Cause they need to see your Supervisor
They must return an item, but they have no receipt
So get off your ass and go find her!

The cell phone is our new "pet"
Sacrificing 'politeness' for air-time
Attention divided while we crash our cars
Might as well have our heads up our behinds!

(fade with repetitive, yet sorrowful-sounding
single piano notes…)

stand in line

get behind—

stand in line!

wait your turn
like everyone else

you know the drill
you get your stuff
then wait in line
to pay for it

no mystery

to this procedure
we've been doing it
all our lives

in single file
behind one another
in front of the other
we all have our place

don't stand beside

or next to me

like you don't know

what's going on

and please don't form

another line

and make believe

you don't see us

we've been here longer
than you have
so get behind—
and stand in line...

and while we're at it
please remove
your shopping cart
that's up my ass

back up a bit
and let me breathe!
the cashier still
must ring me up

I can't move faster
than the person
who got here
before I did

if you're in such a
rush, why not just
leave the line and
steal your food?

there's thirty people
in a line—
you see the line
with your own eyes

then, you walk
right up to the front
and ask someone,
"Is this the line?"

Don't wander 'round
Then try to cut—
You inconsiderate
selfish dung!

Look! The sign says:
"Line Starts Here"
Not "Wherever
You Happen To Be"

— — — — — — — — — — — — — — —

If I were King
I'd make it Law
to exile Those
who cut The Line

contain these
pompous 'jugs & thugs'
upon an island
far away

and let them
wander aimlessly
in search of
clothing, shelter, food

and they can
kill each other for
a string of worms or
dry seaweed…

they'll never have
to wait in line
or ask someone
"Is this the line?"

and when they're ill
they will not have
to wait their turn
to get their meds

and they won't have

to wait to die

no longer doomed

to stand in line.

"Stay The F--k Home!"

I remember the days
When 'time-off' was treasured—
Way back when folks actually
Lived in their homes!

Now, houses are only
For Storage and Day Care
The parties and board games
Of yesteryear, *gone!*

These things we call 'Holidays'
Days we don't work—
Used to be spent with families,
Friends, or alone

But America's a *business*
And Time's Running Out!
You won't get the 'sale price'
Just sitting at home!

So:

Pack the kids in the mini-van
Load those tools in your truck
'cause you *must* purchase lumber
8AM, New Years Day!

Go, set up your bivouac
At 3:00AM
On the Day after Thanksgiving
Just to buy a computer

Save all of your shopping
Until Christmas Eve
Then whine to the manager,
"How come you're *all out?*"

Yes, stumble and bumble
Through this life, dumbfounded
Why can't anybody just
Stay the f—k home?

— — — — — — — — — — — — — —

Stores used to be closed
On Sundays, some Holidays
Even T.V. Stations
Would 'sign-off' in the AM

The Star Spangled Banner
Would play on the screen
Show a big flag waving
You just had to salute

The world used to shut down
And then start up again
Now, Everyone's Running
And they *don't want to stop!*

(…they don't wanna sleep
they don't wanna eat
they don't wanna listen
or have to pay attention…)

Maybe I'm just insane
But I need my sleep
And twenty-four hours off
Every once in a while

No, I don't need office supplies
On Veteran's Day
Or a brand new car
On President's Day

I don't need to be 'moving'
Just because I'm not 'working'
(I've seen and done all that
I've wanted to do)

But to try something *new*
And to try something *now?*
Is what—but a recipe
For aggravation

…leaf blowers in the morning
car alarms blaring all night
The neighbors are either
On vacation or arguing

Houses foreclosing
And jobs laying-off
So you tell me—
"How come stores are still packed?"

I can't tell you 'how'
But I can tell you 'why'—
They're the Only Place Left
That We Have In Our Lives

Where We Can Have 'Tantrums'
Act Out/Dump Grief
To Employees Who Make
A Lot Less Than We Do

Yes, the Store is our Heaven
It's our New Salvation
It's our New Religion
Our Cleansing, Our Fate

It's the Place We Can Go
To Purchase the Goodies
That We'll Only 'Show Off'
Never Have 'Time To Use'

"Gotta go to the store—"
"Gotta purchase, buy more—"
Just in case they 'run out'
And never sell it again!

What will we do then?

Everybody's a Salesman

Can it be marketed?
Can it be sold?
Is it brand new, fresh—
Nostalgic for old?

Can it be packaged?
And put on display?
Can it be ready *today?*

How can we convince you
To purchase our things?
Maybe we should show
A toaster that sings—

A donkey that does math
Or trees that can drive?
Can it be ready by Five?

Can we persuade you to come to our store?
How can we get you to spend more and more?
We all know it's more fun to get than to give
Yes, we'll even sell you a Reason to Live!

Ten pounds of horse-shit
In a five pound bag
Halloween costumes
That dress you in drag

There isn't a product
We haven't seen yet
We can't sell on the internet

If you can come up
With a brand-new idea
Invent a new tool
A cure for diarrhea

Patent/Incorporate
Then mass-produce/sell
You'll no longer suffer
In 'working stiffs hell'!

※※ ※※ ※※ ※※ ※※ ※※ ※※ ※※ ※※ ※※ ※※ ※※ ※※ ※※

Buying and selling is what we all do
Life's just a Transaction, you know this is true!
No matter what you think/know/say/do or feel—
Everyone's a Salesman, so, *let's make a deal!*

The Customer Is Always...

When folks are in "consumer mode"
They purchase, buy and shop
When I serve them in "retail mode"
Da madness nevah stop!

These folks will aggravate you
Till you're ready for a fight
But you bite your tongue and eat shit
'cause The Customer's Always Right!

They don't believe the price tag
When it say $8.99
But no matter how much items cost
Da public groan and whine

Now this behavior, you'd expect
From children, not adults
Folks just end up taller/ruder
Once they get to be grown-ups

They freak out when you tell them
That an item's "out-of-stock"
This is their cue to throw a tantrum—
Disbelief and shock!

They can't read signs or nametags
They just holler "Paper plates?"
No "Excuse me", "Please", or "Could you help?"
No manners as of late!

They want to see the manager
Can't take you on your word
They don't believe a thing you say
You're just a pee-on, turd!

It ain't about the things they buy
When they come to your store
It's where they dump their problems/pain
That's what they come here for

So, cancel the psychiatrist
We're going out tonight—
To abuse department store merchandisers, 'cause
The Customer's Always Right!

In the U.S. of "A.D.D."

Thank God for computers
One thousand channels on TV
We're basking in all
This technology

You say you love it
But it's too much for me
In the U.S. of A.D.D

Plastic phone in your ear
Drive one hundred miles an hour
You got every gadget
But no Personal Power

I'm gonna read the paper
And go take a shower
In the U.S. of A.D.D.

Incidentally—technology
Was supposed to make life easier for you & me

Instead it downsized our personalities
And disintegrated our ability

To pay attention, you see? (Huh?)

I used to go to the movies
And spend time at the mall
These days, it's rare if I go
Anywhere at all

I go to work and go home
Won't even make a phone call
In the U.S. of A.D.D.

I make sure I'm outside
When I light a cigarette
Now, my second-hand smoke
Ain't killed anyone yet

But no one's bitchin' 'bout pollution
From cars, trucks, trains and jets
In the U.S. of A.D.D.

⸻

Ironically—what we need to see
Is escaping our attention quite skillfully

I'm not sure if this is being done deliberately
I'd hate to be the only one to shout 'conspiracy'

(but don't listen to me!)

⸻

I used to be a young man
About twenty years ago
But the older I get
It seems the less that I know

Cast your vote on the
Reality TV Show
In the U.S. of A.D.D.

It's just a matter of time
Before I'm brain-dead
With all this information being beamed
Into my head

Excuse me, sir or madam,
What was that you just said?

In the U.S. of A-D—
U.S. of A-D—
U.S. of A-D—

—DUHHHHHH!—

What You Want

I know what you want…

…for things to go well, of course (who doesn't?)

—but that's rarely the case, is it?

—

…you want a Routine
like the Universe has
the planets spin round
then orbit the sun
the seasons change
(or maybe they don't)
but whatever the case
you want a *Routine.*

—

I know what you want—

Money for Christmas
Candy for Easter
Presents on your Birthday
And Two Weeks Vacation

That raise you were promised
(you deserve it, dag-nabbit!)
A seventy-two degree day
With no clouds in the sky

A money-back guarantee
A college degree
Some toys for the kids
And to lose 20 pounds…

—————————————————————————

…you want Good to Win
and Evil to Lose
(some want the Reverse)
but whatever you choose

I know what you want…

—————————————————————————

I Knew In Advance
How This Whole Thing Would Go
So I Set Up A System
And Put On A Show

First, you Create—
Then, Inculcate—
Then, Perpetuate!
(1.imitate)
(2.emulate)
(3.originate)

—————————————————————————

It wasn't supposed
To occur to you
WHY you want what you want
(but it happened, didn't it?)

I had you distracted
With:

a) Razzle-Dazzle
b) Pomp and Circumstance
c) Ten-Percent Discounts
d) Punitive Discipline
e) Messiahs and Scapegoats
f) Carrots on Sticks
g) Catchy Tunes
h) Special Effects
i) Conspiracy Theories
j) Award Ceremonies

the list goes on, but
I Know What You Want…

— — — — — — — — — — — — — — — —

You Want Nirvana
Heaven
Shangri-La
Peace on Earth

You Want Someone
Who Agrees With You

You Want To Buy One
And Get One Free

You Want Success
And To Get Rick Quick…

— — — — — — — — — — — — — — — —

…but what Everyone Wants
is to Be Set Free
from the Troubles and Traumas
that Make Life Unpleasant

If I Had The Power
Believe me, I'd Do It
For You And For Me—
I'd Set Everyone Free!

But I've No Super-Powers
Just Tricks Up My Sleeve
All That I Can Do
Is Distract and Deceive—

—and hope you *believe*.

Recognize Any Of These Fine Folks?

Someone's Got a Problem

Whether your takin' out the garbage
Or laughin' at a joke
You're gulpin' down a Mountain Dew
Or lightin' up a smoke

The preference hardly matters
Should you choose to stand or sit
You can bet your bottom dollar
Someone's got a problem with it

You could be earnin' lotsa cash
Or maybe unemployed
Even if you have good credit
Somewhere, somebody's annoyed

You may be runnin' here and there
Or have nothin' to do
But I can guarantee that
Someone's got a problem with *you!*

Chorus

Somebody's pissed off no matter what you do or say
Sometimes just showin' up can ruin someone else's day
Why can't we all just get along, and get on with the show
"Well, maybe, yeah, because, but, only if—*I don't think so!*"

You haven't broken any laws
Since 1981
All you wanna do is live yer life
And have some fun

But some folks ain't like you and me
They just won't tip their hat
Instead, they'll knock yours off your head and ask:
"You got a problem with that?"

Issues, drama, trouble,
Upon such, these people thrive
They can't wait to see you suffer
And they hope you don't survive

Who knows what motivates them
Or makes one behave this way?
But I'll bet you your whole paycheck
Someone's got a problem today

Bridge

Somewhere in every neighborhood
There's someone in a room
Trapped behind a television
Prisoners of gloom

Their heads full of ideas
On the way things ought to be
Shocked and stunned to find their thoughts
Don't match "reality"

Well, someone's got to answer for this
Someone has to pay
The anger flowing though their veins
Will manifest today

They've got to find a scapegoat
For themselves they cannot blame
They cannot sleep unless they're causing
Someone else's shame…

Now it used to be that people
Tried to live the Golden Rule
They understood that jealousy and
Envy bred a fool

Not these days, buddy, no sir-ee
To much we must attend
We can't let down our guard, cause
Someone's got a problem, My friend

Our lives go by but in a flash
To Earth, return our bones
We're underground, yes, 6 feet down
No longer Smith or Jones

And no one knows the day or hour
That they are to pass—

So before I go
I just wanna let you know
If someone's got a problem
They can stick it up
My cold, dead, ass…

Someone's got a problem
Whether you are fat or thin
Someone's got a problem
Whether you go out or in

Someone's got a problem
Whether you are young or old
Someone's got a problem
If the weather's hot or cold

Someone's got a problem
If you marry or divorce
Someone's got a problem
If you saddle up your horse

Someone's got a problem if
If you buy a home or rent
Someone's got a problem with
Your attic or basement

Someone's got a problem
If your pet's a cat or dog
Someone's got a problem
If your pet's a bird or frog

Someone's got a problem
If you have no pets at all
Someone's got a problem
If you don't give them a call

Someone's got a problem
Whether you are straight or gay
Someone's got a problem with
Somebody else today

Someone's got a problem
With the postman and the cop
Someone's got a problem
Will the problems ever stop?

Someone's got a problem
Cause their coupons didn't take
They didn't save .03 cents on toilet paper
Or a cake

Someone's got a problem
Cause their taxes are too high
Or their flight is 15 minutes late
And no one tells them why

Someone's got a problem
With the way you cut your hair
Or the fact that you arrive at
Every place once you get there

Someone's got a problem
If your doin' what your taught
And someone's got a problem
With those 20 fish you caught...

Some folks just can't help but makin'
All their problems yours
They've got the time to place your crimes
Above their daily chores

They'll offer unsolicited advice
They'd never heed
They'll disagree with both sides
Cause its arguments they need

(Someone's got a problem
cause the movie ran too long
someone's got a problem
and they wrote it in a song!)

It seems, these kind were put here
On this earth to cause us pain
They'll gripe about the drought, next year
They'll bitch about the rain...

I'm Important!

"Attention, everyone—
All hands on deck!"
Roll out the Red Carpet
'cause I'm On the Premises

My high heels a-clackin'
My cell phones a-ringin'
My business suit's glowin'
And my teeth are a-sparklin'!

I demand satisfaction
I deserve my own way
I demand a recount,
A rain check, a rebate!

What are you, blind?
Didn't you see me coming?
I gave you the clues
And over-emphasized gestures!

My posture, my stance
My intimidating glare
The look in my eyes that states,
"You owe me something!"

C'mon, piss-ant, *serve me!*
Let's go, bend your ear—
Listen to my Life Story
And my Latest Adventures!

My new car is large
And radiant and LOUD!
In this world full of losers
I stand out from the crowd!

But, that's My Whole Objective
And will be 'till I die—
So, come on, people, serve me, because
I'm Important!

My Life Sucks, and You're Gonna Pay!

I wake up each and every day

Just miserable—what can I say?

My anger, always on display

'cause my life sucks and you're gonna pay!

I cannot hide my misery

(a scapegoat always works for me)

This ain't how I thought Life Would Be

(I choose my victims randomly)

I stick my finger in your face

I blame you for my fall from grace

I'm pissed 'cause I can't have my way

Yes, my life sucks, and you're gonna pay!

If I knew how to Make Things Right

I wouldn't do so—just for spite!

Instead, I'll torture you until

You're ready to write out your will!

No matter what you do or say

The "Nasty Life" is the game I play

Wish you the worst all seven days

'cause my life sucks, and you're gonna pay!

Folks I Wished I Hadn't The Pleasure of Knowing

Drug Dealer Boyfriend
Company Thief
Restless Leg Syndrome
You Got No Relief

Attention Span Zero
But you think you're a thug
Real fuckin' gangsters
Fill your skull with a slug

Parking lot crazies
With Their 'Beggars Card'
Go out and get a job, man—
It ain't dat hard!

You lookin in da mirror
'cause your hair's turning gray
Your Old Man calling you
Fifty times a day (Shit!)

You think you're a bad-ass
And you think I'm a jerk
But how tough can you be
When you don't wanna work?

Eighty pounds overweight
Attitude sucks
Born-Again Asshole
Can't unload the trucks

You'd better incorporate
Or Your Biggest Fear
Will manifest itself
Within your life this year!

I wonder what problems
Come with that 'pretty face'?
Sorry to have met you
Time for a new workplace!

I Just Want To Go To Prison

I'm a fuckin' tough guy
Don't you mess with me
'Cause I'll cut off your balls
and make a Scrotum Fricassee

I can talk and brag about
The gangster life I'm in
'cause I just want to go
to prison!

I spit on you with disrespect
I treat you like a jerk
Don't ask me to do nuthin'
'cause I just don't wanna work!

I'll scare you with my mean face
And the tattoo's on my skin
'cause I just want to
go to prison!

Right now, I'm workin' nine-to-five
But this won't last forever
Eventually, I'll get arrested

I'm planning my next caper
(got it all right here on paper!)
Commit my crime
& do my time
The Legal System Tested!

I'm a real bad-boy
So get out of my way
No matter if my mommy
Drive me to work every day

OK, I'm just a *'wanna-be'*
But someday, I'll Get In—
'cause I just wanna
go to prison!

No, there's no place for me,
In Society—
I know I'm better off
In prison!

"…and the voice over the music says"—

(…man, I can't wait to learn how to make shanks, have anal sex, brew toilet wine, and go before parole boards! Just like they do on TV! You'll see—I'll live my *dream* someday…)

Guess Who Doesn't Give a Shit?

Guess who doesn't give a shit?
Not me buddy, no siree!
It's not my job, man, get away from me!
'cause I just don't give a shit!

I don't wanna fix the environment
No sense speakin' out against the government
Don't wanna hear about your kids or family
'cause I just don't give a shit!

What did you expect?
A World that's Fair & Kind?
Better grabba holda your neck—
And pull your head outta your behind!

I don't care about inflation,
Pollution or crime
I'll let you do the worryin', 'cause
I ain't got the time

Quit tellin' me your troubles
And just deal with it—
'cause I
just don't give a shit!

Don't give me your religion
Or your self-help talk
Your political-correctness
Or your bad-ass walk

I ain't intimidated
Or impressed, you see—
So just *get the hell*
Away from me!

I'll run you off the road
If you're driving too slow
Kick you in the balls
Just to watch you turn blue
Ram my face smack
Between your tits
'cause I just don't give a shit!

⸻ ⸻ ⸻ ⸻ ⸻ ⸻ ⸻ ⸻ ⸻ ⸻ ⸻

You sayin' I'm harsh
You sayin' I'm cruel
They didn't teach behavior
Like this in school

Well, out here in the Real World
There ain't no rules
Just laws to make money
Off of 'getting caught'!

So go ahead, be an asshole
Or a filthy slob
If your salary permits
Be a stuck-up snob

Do whatever you want
And be done with it—

'cause I just don't give a—
just don't give a—

just don't give a shit-TAH!"

(…nobody cares…)

If It Hurts *That Much*...

If it pains you to see
Smiling faces and glee
If it's too much to bear
When you see someone care
If you just can't stand
People lending a hand
If it makes you feel ill
When you witness goodwill...

Why not run headfirst
Into the nearest brick wall?
Jump off a tall building
When you land, paint the pavement?
Stand in front of a bus
Or an oncoming train
Set yourself on fire
While we "sing in the rain"!

But whatever you do
(whatever's best for you)
please, do it somewhere
far, far, far away

Don't ruin our lives
Just 'cause yours is a wreck
Don't spoil our food
'cause you can't stand yours

Eat your pain, if you're hungry
Drink your tears if you're sad
Eat some shit for dessert
Till you go crazy, mad!

Then we'll lock you away
You can spend every day
In a small room, chained to your bed,
High on meds...

(will *this* satisfy you?)

You Can't Please 'Em, So Don't Even Try

It's come to the point
> Where I can't care much longer

About people who don't care
> (Yet demand that *I should*!)

These hypocrites—idiots!
> What imbeciles—fools!

Are they so deceived
> To believe I *believe them*?

They're giving instructions
> Designed to confuse

They're drawing up blueprints
> With defects and faults...

Do they *want* things to fail?

So that *they* can fix them?

And then take the credit

While you foot the blame?

They won't accept ignorance

As a bargain or plea

(But 'ignorant' is what

they must want us to be!)

Because when you Make Sense

And use Intelligence

You can bet that your punishment's

Lying in wait!

━━ ━━ ━━ ━━ ━━ ━━ ━━ ━━ ━━ ━━ ━━ ━━ ━━ ━━ ━━

Your Reason annoys them

Your Truth brings them pain

They demand "explanations"

(and then, they *ignore* them!)

                  I can't care much longer
But I'm hardly depressed
              In fact, I'm quite happy
Content, and at ease
              If the World Wants Results
They need not consult me
              Their brains and their limbs
Work as well as mine do
              And, as I'm expected
To "serve" and to "answer"
              To "work" and "earn keep"
Just like Everyone Else...

━━ ━━ ━━ ━━ ━━ ━━ ━━ ━━ ━━ ━━ ━━ ━━ ━━ ━━ ━━

- When the tantrums begin, and folks scream for their rights
- When the double-talk rolls off the tips of their tongues
- When the pompous and pious come out of their caves
- When the ugliness makes itself manifest, known
- When the once-kind are damaged beyond full repair
- When the ones that can lend a hand turn up their nose
- Once Transgression's Accomplished, there's No Turning Back…

You Just Can't Please 'Em, So Don't Even Try…

An
Interview
With
The
Author

An Interview With The Author

Conducted by Dick Bonerhead, Columnist for *Rudeweek*
August, 2008 Issue

00000 30000 30000 30000 00000 30000 30000 00000 00000 00000 30000 00000 00000 00000

TELL US A LITTLE BIT ABOUT DAVID Q. TAGUE...
If I do, this will prove an extremely short interview. How about I tell you even more?

O.K. THEN, LET'S TALK ABOUT "INANE BALDERDASH".
Gladly! It's the follow-up to my first collection of writings; *Miscellaneous Hullabaloo, Collected Works 1992—2007,* and I just began editing/rewriting yesterday. I should have it ready for mass-consumption by 2009.

WHAT IS IT THAT MAKES YOU WRITE?
Usually a pen and some paper.

MORE SUCCINCTLY, WHAT IS YOUR MOTIVATION FOR WRITING?
When I talk to people in person, in real life, and in real time, I usually end up:
  1) Boring them
  2) Pissing them off
  3) Talking so much I cause them to be late for previously scheduled, yet unavoidably painful dental procedures.
However, when I say the *same exact things* on the printed page, or sing them from behind a guitar, people say:
  a) Wow, you're an author?
  b) Wow, great music!
  c) Thanks, Dave, your books/songs helped me get through a recently scheduled yet unavoidably painful dental procedure.

121

WHEN DID YOU FIRST START TO EXPRESS YOURSELF ON PAPER?
In High School English Classes. Remember how they'd force you to write 200-word compositions on topics such as "If I Were In Charge of the World" or "What I Would Do With A Million Dollars?" All that "What If" stuff. One teacher was cool and gave us (the students) an "option" to write whatever *we* wanted one day, and that's where I took off.

CAN YOU REMEMBER THAT FIRST ESSAY?
I'll never forget it—entitled "Santa Claus is the Anti-Christ", I surmised that since Ole Kris Kringle knew where every "present-deserving" child on the entire earth lived, and could deliver their non-earned gifts across the globe within a measly 4-6 hour time frame, that *he alone* had the power to bring about Armageddon. Let U.P.S., Fed Ex, or the U.S. Postal Service try that trick!

WHAT GRADE DID YOU GET ON THIS PIECE?
I can't recall, but I do remember that after the teacher read the essay out loud to the whole class, ten kids converted to Judaism within the following two weeks.

HOW ABOUT YOURSELF? DO YOU HAVE ANY RELIGIOUS BELIEFS?
Not since I have been officially cured of "Romantic Delusia".

WHAT IS "ROMANTIC DELUSIA"?
It is a state of mind that creates a good mood based on false hopes. Once, however, all illusions have been shattered within one's belief system, they are free to create their own happiness, based on reason, logic, and personal effort.

HOW LONG DID YOU SUFFER FROM THIS AILMENT?
For about 39 years. I turn 42 today, so I have been "Delusion-Free" for about three years now.

DO YOU FEAR A "RELAPSE"?
Not after gathering/re-reading all the pieces for *Inane Balderdash,*
which, in my mind, will prove the Ultimate Antidote for anyone else
suffering the same affliction. Hey—how about a "Happy Birthday" or
"Congratulations"?

(Dick Bonerhead, fighting to stay awake, requests a two-hour break
from the interview for a few stiff drinks and a nap. David Q. gladly
obliges, himself going out to smoke half a carton of Marlboro
Cigarettes and erase all the "missed calls" clogging up his cell phone
menu.)

Part Two

WHO ARE YOUR FAVORITE AUTHORS?
Ray Bradbury, George Orwell, and Kurt Vonnegut, to start. If I had my way, it would be <u>mandatory</u> that *Every American* read the Following "Trifecta" sometime within their lives:
1) *Fahrenheit 451*
2) *1984 (or Animal Farm)*
3) *Breakfast of Champions*

WHAT MAKES YOU FEEL SO STRONGLY ABOUT THIS?
Anyone taking the time to investigate these three masterpieces will get a glimpse as to How Da World Works, and Why Their Lives Don't. These novels wonderfully explain the mechanics of Oppression and Nonsense, used in these stories (and in Real Life) to prevent human beings from reaching their *full potential*, should they decide to accept such a mission.

YOU ARE BEGINNING TO SOUND LIKE A SELF-HELP AUTHOR.
In that genre, I recommend *You Can Work Your Own Miracles* by Napoleon Hill. Most self-help books are more *inspirational* than *practical*—you've basically got a "coach on paper" fueling your own particular brand of *Romantic Delusia*, telling you that you can become Rich, Good-Looking, Successful, Sexy, and Run the Entire Universe if you just use put your Latent, Magic, Subconscious Powers to work for you—and you can accomplish all this while overeating, in your sleep, and during a haircut!

DO YOU ASPIRE TO ACHIEVE THE SAME GREATNESS AS THESE AUTHORS?
I wouldn't mind matching their *sales!*

THEN AGAIN, THESE WERE WRITERS OF FICTION & WISDOM—YOU, ON THE OTHER HAND, COMPOSE POETRY, SONGS, AND ESSAYS...

Yes. As someone who is used to writing songs, I am used to "getting to the point" within 3-5 minutes. A Novel is a Long Story with a Main Character who is in Pursuit of Something, and, after experiencing Numerous Escalating Obstacles, Trials, and Conflicts, makes a Critical Choice, the actions of which either Get Them The Thing They Desire, or Don't. Some people can make their point in two hundred pages, others can make them in two. And *your* point is?

WELL, POETRY RARELY SELLS AS WELL AS FICTION...DO YOU SEE YOURSELF ATTEMPTING AN ACTUAL NOVEL SOMEDAY, OR JUST CONTINUING TO HACK, UH, PUBLISH SHORT, SEEMINGLY UNRELATED PIECES? (BURP)
Seems like you've got a good "buzz" goin', and I'd hate to interrupt it—can we break for a few beers and get back to this interview later?

HEY! I'M *SUPPOSED TO BE ASKIN' THE QUESTIONS!*
(Dick Bonerhead frowns as David Q. goes to the fridge and pulls out two cans of Budweiser.)

ALLRIGHT, IF YOU INSIST...
(Crack! Slurp—Gurgle...)

Part Three

*HEY, MAN—THANKS FOR TREATIN' ME TO LUNCH! WHAT
DID WE HAVE TO EAT AGAIN? (HICCUP)*
We didn't. (David Q. breaks wind.) We just *drank.*

*OH, YEAH! IT WAS THOSE PEOPLE NEXT TO US THAT WERE
EATIN'! SURE SMELLED GOOD, THOUGH!*
Did you have more answers, a-huh-huh-huh, questions for me?

YEAH, YEAH, LEMME GET THE LIST...
Lemme get more beer! (falls off chair, laughing...)

*OK, OK, HERE WE GO—(COUGHS, UNCRUMBLES LIST FROM
POCKET)—HOW DO YOU COME UP WITH IDEAS FOR YOUR
STUFF?*
I find the nearest brick wall and run headfirst into it. After regaining
consciousness, I either grab a guitar or a pen/paper, and I'm off to the
races!

*WHEN YOU WRITE SONGS, DO YOU HEAR THE MUSIC
FIRST, OR THE LYRICS?*
I usually can't hear anything for days after this particular ordeal. So, I
usually hit the nearest Dairy Barn, stock up on beer/smokes, hole up
in the apartment for a few weeks, and Bingo! Here's your new songs/
manuscript/whatever!

*ARE YOU THAT DEPENDENT ON SUBSTANCES TO PRODUCE
RESULTS?*
On the contrary—if it weren't for me, those "substances" would just
rot on the shelves! How does that help our hurting economy?

*IS IT TRUE THAT YOU TURNED DOWN PLAYBOY'S REQUEST
FOR AN INTERVIEW TO DO OUR MAGAZINE INSTEAD?*
No, your gang offered me a year's supply of Turtle-Wax and Two Free
Years of Playboy for doing this interview with you.

WHAT MAKES "DAVID Q." TICK?
Stopwatches, bombs, and Lyme's Disease.

HOW DO YOU TREAT YOUR FANS?
Not as well as my air conditioners, but, but BUT—ade-adequately enough to keep 'em selling at my garage sales.

DO YOU HAVE ANY ADVICE FOR UP AND COMING NEW WRITERS?
Not really, but I do have some uninteresting suggestions for the more famous/established authors.

IF THERE WERE ONE THING YOU COULD CHANGE ABOUT YOURSELF, WHAT WOULD IT BE?
My underwear.

IS THERE A "DAVID Q." MESSAGE?
Yes, on my Answering Machine.

(Dick Bonerhead clicks off the tape recorder, and falls face-first into the coffee table. As David Q. gets up to take a 'well-needed' piss, Dick asks, "Hey, can I tack-on those pieces you wrote on the back of the restaurant place-mats to the end of this interview?"
David Q. replies, "You can wipe your ass with them for all I care!")

Do You Suffer From "Crapplebee's Disease"?

You've heard right, comrade—and epidemic of stupendous proportions is sweeping the Long Island Bar & Restaurant Scene! At this very moment, hundreds of Young American Males are SUFFERING—not from V.D., E.D., or H.D.T.V.—

—no, my friend, 'tis a fate much, much worse—they have acquired the infamous "Crapplebee's Disease"! (OH MY GOD!)

SYMPTOMS:

MENU DYSLEXIA: Inability to decipher any courses in menu except those listed under "alcoholic beverages". Causes undue stress attempting to read the "Men's Room" sign.

POTATO SKIN FEVER: Customer's compulsory non-stop gorging on these tasty treats causes bloating, spontaneous insults, and uncontrollable passing of wind in the presence of college-age waitresses.

JOKE-AHOLISM: Blithering bubble-heads plop their fat asses on a barstool all evening and do nothing but drink, laugh loudly, and enjoy themselves. This behavior disrupts those patrons/families seated at neighboring dinner tables whom are sincerely trying to remain miserable/chew their food simultaneously.

BI-POLAR BARMAID DISORDER: Seriously deluded "regulars" develop the twisted logic that they actually have a chance to "score" with one of the many available (or not!) "Crapplebees Beauties". Poor waitresses/barmaids are subjected to endless come-ons, marriage proposals, stale jokes, as well as unwanted invitations to Pet Funerals, Divorce Proceedings, or the back of a 1957 Chevy (restored).

WHAT YOU CAN DO

If you are a frequent Crapplebee's Customer and find yourself suffering from any of the above-documented symptoms, take the following actions immediately, lest the disease progress to the further/final stages of 1) CRAPPLE-BALLS, 2) PARKING-LOT DEMENTIA, or 3) BAR-TAB DEFECIT SYNDROME!

a) Admit you are powerless over Crapplebee's
b) Go to other bars and drink twice as much
c) Stay home and watch "Weather Channel" reruns
d) Call up old enemies you haven't fought with in awhile
e) Seek the wise counsel of a local loan shark/stripper
f) Spend quality-time in the 4th dimension
g) Ahh, screw it! I'm going back to Crapplebees tomorrow, who am I kidding!

Drunkard's Lament

Let's go somewhere for food and drink
Says "Q." to "Dickie B."
On 107, Nassau
Stands the Famous "Crapplebees"!

Who knew what they'd encounter
As they entered through the door
Would they wait long for a table?
Shit—two barstools they did score!

"Who are these guys?" employees thought
"They drink & laugh real loud!"
"Life ain't that good!" yelled someone
from the Angry Dinner Crowd

So much for having "too much fun"
Now get down on your knees
And hope to Hell you don't become
A slave of "Crapplebees"!

⸻

Dear Dick: Thanks for the interview, if either of us remember it
actually happened by the time we sober up. —*David Q.*

Pals
&
Scenes
From
The
"David
Q."
Playground

The "Raynor-Horse" (A Tribute)

(…gallop-trot…gallop-trot!)

(Gallop-Trot! GALLOP! TROT!)

Feedbag——mailbag——ballbag——RAYNOR-HORSE!

Listen to this story
'Cause I guarantee it's true—
It's all about the "Raynor-Horse"
Inside the "Postal Zoo"…

…when he was just a pony
A donkey bit his tail
So he kicked him in the ass
And refused to give him mail!

Now he's all grown up
With a family of his own
Inside their stable:
Cable, internet and phone!

He's a Shop Steward
With a saddle and a mane
He doin' everything
To keep from going insane!

His Great Grand-dad
Was in the Pony Express
Now the Raynor-Horse delivers
For the U.S.P.S.!

It sure ain't easy
What the Raynor-Horse do—
Bringing magazines
And bills and checks to you

But he's One Tough Stallion
No, he'll never complain—
He'll deliver mail
In snow-hail-sleet-and-rain!

(...gallop-trot-gallop-trot...)
(...drop-da-letters-in-da-box!)

Raynor-Horse work so hard
You'd think he's immortal—
He work so many jobs
You'd think he owns a "time-portal"—

—To accomplish all he do
and dat his claim to fame—
Everybody on Long Island
Know his name!

He drive da soda truck
And then—security guard—
He make da kids dinner
Then rake leaves in da yard

He da best provider
Dat a man can be
Well-loved and respected
By his family!

(…gallop-trot-gallop-trot…)
(…newspapers at da qwick-stop!)

 A Salute to the "Raynor-Horse"
Is only right
You steal his sugar cubes
You in for a fight!

He never unsteady
Never veer off course
Ladies and gentlemen, we now present to you…

The Raynor-Horse!

Da "Postmaster Bear-Hug"

Feeling down, and kinda depressed?
Your job ain't fun, your life is a mess?
Don't give up—there's relief in sight—
A "Postmaster Bear-Hug" will set you right!

Forget "chiropractic", or drug therapy
The Downtown P.O. is the place you gotta be
For an attitude adjustment, or a pat on the back—
A "Postmaster Bear-Hug" get you back on track!

How did everything get so complicated?
Sometimes, I just can't "get a grip"—
I'm just a young punk, tryin' to Get It Right The First Time
No matter what, I always slip! Trip! BLIP!

Agitated—no place to go?
Your woman won't give you no "rodeo"?
Your wallet is empty, and so is your head—
(A "Postmaster Bear-Hug" wake you up from the dead!)

All and all, sum it up in one breath—
Man put on this Earth—and sentenced to *Death!*
No sense feeling down, 'bout your Eventual Fate—

Get a "Postmaster Bear-Hug"—BEFORE IT'S TOO LATE!

(Author's Note: I actually worked for a postmaster who bear-hugged
us every morning. It built morale amongst employees, so they shipped
him away.)

Triple Joe Coffee

He big and he mean
He don't take no shit
He da bouncer and da lead guitarist
And he lovin' it

He ain't Einstein,
Travis Tritt or Brad Pitt
He Triple Joe Coffee…

His size and his mass
Make Godzilla look small
You stand next to him
You only two feet tall

His scrotum as big
As an NFL Football
He Triple Joe Coffee…

Joker, Joker, and a Triple!
Top 5 Answers are On The Board!
Paul Lynde to Block, Charlie Weaver to Win!
Mess with Triple Joe Coffee, you gonna pay for your sins!

"Oversized Jim Mocha" is just a wimp
He's a softy, *imposter*!—Send him up as a blimp!
While the "Raynor-Horse" handin' out mail to the pimp
Da barmaid, she droolin, and walk with a limp!

You goin' out drinkin' on Saturday Night
You rock and you roll and get into a fight
"Triple Joe" stops his solo and heads straight for you—
Throw you out on your ass, like they pay him to do!

———————————————————————

[<u>Your Best Bet?</u> Stay home and drink.]

Hap-Bidda-Boo

I've come to a conclusion
After years of contemplation
A lifetime full of confusion
Non-stop years of aggravation

Searching for perfect solutions
Focusing my concentration
But it's all been a delusion
Now I have a *revelation*...

The Answer to Life
Is contained in Just Three Words
They may just ring familiar
Or like nothing you have heard

So say them to yourself
Repeat them every day
Then watch all your troubles
Dissolve and fade away

Are you ready, my friend
To start a life anew?
Repeat after me—
Hap-Bidda-Boo!

You've been assigned a mantra
The one that holds the key
Yes, "Hap-Bidda-Boo"
Brings peace to all, you see!

It frees you from all worries
And settles all disputes
It conquers opposition
Brings resolve to long lawsuits!

―――――――――――――――――

It answers all your questions
And it helps you see the truth
You needn't be a genius
It don't take a 'super-sleuth'

To say these three little words
Just like you're gonna do
Repeat after me—
"Hap-Bidda-Boo!"

"Jimmeh"

Everybody "Jimmeh"
Jimmeh's Everyone
Man, you know dat Jimmeh
He a buncha fun

Everybody "Jimmeh"
Jimmeh's Everywhere
Nab him for an autograph
Or a few locks of his hair

Everybody "Jimmeh"
A hard man to track down
If you can't get in touch with him
Don't start to cry or frown

Everybody "Jimmeh"
Jimmeh, he da Man
If no one else can 'handle' it,
Trust me, Jimmeh can

Jimmeh at da racetrack
Jimmeh at da game
We all call him Jimmeh
Because dat be his name

Jimmeh's God and Santa Claus
He's your Aunt Martha, too
Jimmeh end up Everywhere
No matter what he do

Now you see him, now you don't
Dat Jimmeh, man, he tricky
He kiss da girls and make 'em fly
But don't leave them no hickey

Everyone love Jimmeh,
He famous, known worldwide
It make a person happy
Knowing Jimmeh by his side.

"DASHPACK!"

I wanted so badly
To tell you that I loved you
So I wrote you a letter
And I sent it in a *DASHPACK!*

Didn't Fed-Ex it
Didn't UPS it
Hadda get it there fast
So I sent it in a *DASHPACK!*

I'm driving like a maniac all over town
The upside-down smile on my face is a frown
I ain't had no lovin' since I don't know when
So open up my Dashpack
And let's start smoochin' *AGAIN!*

Information traveling
At the speed of sound
Happy-smiling-faces
Take a look around
They didn't win the lotto
Or a Contest First Prize
I can tell you what they got
From just the look in their eyes

They got a—

(spell it out with me, gang!)

D------A------S------H------P------A------C------K!

"DASHPACK!"

58 Scherer Street Freedom

You thought you had nuthin'
When you 'had it made'
Ain't got enough sense
To know when you been 'paid'

The "Good Ole Times"
Have vanished and gone
You used to be smart
Now, you're a moron

Your happiness lie
In "Studio Three"
But you locked it up
And swallowed the key

What manner or method
Is there left to try?
Technology has
Removed every "Why?"

Now watch as new tenants
Move into this place
Observe as the life
Disappears from your face

58 Scherer Street Freedom
Is What I Threw Away
If I had a lick-o-common-sense
I'd still be there today.

(for Shirley and Edward)

Cowboy Chris

My name is Cowboy Chris
I have to take a piss
So 'scuse me while I hide behind this cactus

I loves da girls, I hugs 'em and I squeeze 'em
I kiss 'em all night, it's my aim to please 'em
And when I go to church, I'm a "Cowboy Baptist"!

Now I love livin' in da Wild Wild West
Drinkin' and gunfightin' is what I do best
You mess wit' me, you'll be wearing your ass for a hat

I ain't no genius, but I ain't no dope
I can shoe any horse, make a lasso with rope
You screw wit me, you'll be R.I.P. and dat's dat!

Lemme tell ya a story that once happened to me
I was hangin' from a noose around a big ole tree
When an Indian Squaw shot me down with a bow and arrow

She saved my life, and for this I was grateful
The town done wronged me, for that I was hateful
You see, I was once the Sheriff at Big Wheelbarrow!

They accused me of dippin' into funds from da bank
And some folks complained 'bout all the beer that I drank
So they set me up, and they hung me out to *die...*

But that Indian Gal, who lived in a teepee
Was cross-eyed, and aimed that arrow right at my pee-pee
So I shit my britches and kissed my ass goodbye!

His name is Cowboy Chris
He has to take a piss
So excuse him while he hides behind that cactus

He loves da girls, he hugs 'em and he squeeze 'em
He kiss 'em all night, it's his aims to please 'em
Thurston Howell the 3rd was played by Jim Backus!

Lucky fer me, there was a wind passin' by
Unfortunately tossed some bird shit into my eye
But it blew dat arrow smack above my head

I landed balls first as I thumped to da ground
I squealed like a sissy, but then I came around
As that Indian Gal brought me back from the dead!

Now in these times I live, you gonna find it rare
That anyone wearin' feathers in their hair
Gonna help you out as you're takin' their land away

But I knew right on the spot—made an Instant Decision
Didn't need no coaxin', or to see any visions
I proposed to her, and we got married the next day!

My name is Cowboy Chris
It now hurts when I piss
So excuse me while I shy behind this cactus

No more fussin' and foolin' wit different gals all da time
Watch out, Big Wheelbarrow—you gonna pay for your crime
*If they think they can outshoot me, they gonna need **practice!***

"Son's-a-Crap!"

It don't rhyme with "Bidda"
It don't rhyme with "Hap"
It's now Your Favorite Catch-Phrase—
Here it comes: "Son's-a-crap!"

A "million-dollar winner"?
To check, lift up the flap—
But it says, "Sorry—try again!"
And you say: "Son's-a-crap!"

"Come here, child," says Santa Claus
"Yes, sit here on my lap!"
Proceed to pull off his fake beard
And holler: "Son's-a-crap!"

Another night of drinkin'
Order two "Tall Buds" on tap
"Oh shit! I left my wallet home!"
You pal pays—"Son's-a-crap!"

When toddlers misbehave
Parents give their tush a slap
When teens use drugs or get knocked up
Their folks yell "Son's-a-crap!"

Hey! Check out that British Bloke!
A Good-Ole English Chap!
He stammers: "Bollocks! Bloody hell!"
Instead of "Son's-a-crap!"

You're feelin' kinda groggy
And decide to take a nap
Next time, don't do so while you're driving—
CRASH! "Son's-a-crap!"

You're caught in a dilemma
An unfortunate mishap—
One poem short a chapter
What do you write? *"Son's-a-crap!"*

Not Me (Canine Conundrum)

I never thought I'd see the day
When my poor dog would pass away
She misses him, not me
She's going to the cemetery

"Milkbone Memories"
Excessive scratching due to fleas
She misses him, not me—
Not me!

She leaves T-Bones
By the headstone
I'm stuck eating quiche

Clothes no longer
Pressed/ironed
As she clings to that "leash'

I said, "Let's go down
To the pound
And get another hound!"

I'll bet she wishes
It was me
Instead of him
Who was no longer around!

Don't get me wrong, you see
I really miss my canine friend
I always thought that we would be
Together till the end

The Mrs. misses all the times
The three of us would play
Now she can't function anymore
She'll have to 'go away'…

⸺ ⸺ ⸺ ⸺ ⸺ ⸺ ⸺ ⸺ ⸺ ⸺ ⸺ ⸺ ⸺ ⸺ ⸺

I drive by the Asylum
Hoping she's alright
The doctor's claim she still hears 'barking'
Each and every night

They say a dog's a
Man's Best Friend
But women love 'em, too

The only thing I don't miss
Is cleaning up
That doggie-doo!

⸺ ⸺ ⸺ ⸺ ⸺ ⸺ ⸺ ⸺ ⸺ ⸺ ⸺ ⸺ ⸺ ⸺ ⸺

Playing catch with frisbees
Getting shots down at the vet
Three years since Fido died
And still, my wife is not home yet

I wonder if it's worth the pain

To get another pet?

jibber-jabberin' (for my pal Doug)

you flappin' yo lips

but it justa buncha nonsense

you speakin' a language

I don't understand

You hummin' and hawin'

You nuttin' but hog-jawin'

I don't wanna

Hear it no mo'!

You sputterin', spatterin'
(none of it flatterin')

Piano Teeth chatterin'
can't hear a word!

You preachin' from pulpits
Of pallets and crates

You're Nick-at-Nite Sermon is
makin' me *late!*

sentences/syllables
what do they mean?
They all out of synch
Can't you get to da point?

it's all over—all over
it is *me* you betray
When you stand there just
Jibber-jabberin' all day!

You'd better invest
In a good dictionary
You keep talkin' backwards
You'll live in reverse!

You no Cool Hand Luke
You no Liberty Valance
You a Stumble-Bum Clipboard
Who screwed up my run!

Can't talk your way out of it
Sentences mixed—
Syntax inaudible
What did you say?

My deliveries, late—
You a Jerk-in-da-Box!
You a fool, flabbergasted
By pronouns and verbs!

Guess I'll take my leave
Get my rig on the road
Gotta meet up with "J. M."
Out in Rockingham

But the next time I come here
To pick up a load
You'd better be *ready*
Not fulla excuses

No more mumbo-jumbo
No more fumblin' for words
No more blither & blather
No mo' talkin' trash!

Cause if I gotta hear
 Any more of your
  Jibber-jabberin—

  I'll shatter that glass jaw of yours into dust!

Rough Cull (a short play)

David Q:

"Jiffy-Pop Head" in my rear-view mirror
Bitchin' babe in my front seat
"Ronco Erection Surpressor" on backorder
multitudes of sins at my feet

"What am I gonna do, Johnny?
What am I gonna do?
How am I to deal with it, Johnny?
I need an answer from you!"

Johnny G.:

Thirty-one years of tribulation
Still, you're standin' tall!
Ten years of "postal aggravation"
You survived it all

You're gonna be O.K., David
Trust in Johnny G.
You're gonna be just fine, David
Take this advice from me

Tony B.:

D.Q.—this is Tony B.
Your good pal, the 'consigliere'
Management don't care 'bout you
That's why the Union pay me!

I'm here to tell you, David Q.
Your fight is not in vain
Make a "rough cull" of your accomplishments
Before you go insane!!!

<u>Supporting</u> <u>Cast</u> <u>Members:</u>	Rough cull Rough cull Weed out the disease Make yourself Indestructible

Rough cull
Rough cull
You're the matador
Not the bull
Unbelievable!

Rough cull
You're responsible
Not a ship
Without a hull
Do not fret or fume or mull

Rough cull
You're valuable
Not expendable
Make that "rough cull!"

(...it's <u>nice</u> to have *friends*...)

zip—zap—crappo!

da ladies turn me down again
rivals now, were pals back when
worryin' 'bout when the world gonna end
zip—zap—crappo!

I yell *"Blip!"* and scream *"BAYOUP!"*
One Big Bomber, Two Cups-a-Soup
Listen to the gossip and the Latest Scoop
zip—zap—crappo!

{nuthin' much make sense to me
so I invent these "phrases", see?
To help cope with the life I'm in
Commence—Let Da Games Begin!}

4-track and a drum machine
(distort guitars, feed vocals clean)
to science, I donate my spleen
zip—zap—crappo!

Whenceforth, why, and hitherto
Here I go again— *"Hap-Bidda-Boo!"*
I'm insane—with naught to do
zip—zap—crappo!

{I watch TV and rot my head
I read (my favorite authors—dead!)
I sleep but never get no rest
I always fail to pass the "test"}

These days, a word don't mean a thing
You drivin' and your cell phone ring
Someday, everybody will sing—
zip—zap—crappo!

Wink Rattlesnake's Stationary Carnivale

"Buffalo Cheese" @ EuroNews.net

The history of Buffalo Cheese begins in 1879, when a Romanian Farmer named Count Spedlak Furricane suffered famine for his labors during a terrible season of drought and brush fires.

Running out of private stock gathered over the years, the Count, his wife, and his 15 children began to ration, then to starve.

Hardly a family of sissies, they came up with an idea to have a "Food Fair", inviting peoples from miles around to his small town of Offoffmania, and told them all to bring a dish of their choice, to be judged in a "contest".

It took the Count six weeks on the back of a water buffalo, riding through the countryside, to spread the word from home to home.

Stopping at a nearby tavern on his last day before heading home, he ran into the famed German Explorer Reichstagg Pricetag, former "borscht" magnate. After many lagers and double the Polish Jokes, a slurred, yet barely audible conversation ensued.

"Do you like cheese?" asked Pricetag.

"I love cheese!" said Furricane.

"I'll bet you make a killing on Buffalo Cheese, then. (Burp!)"

"*Buffalo Cheese?* I usually make cheese from Cows Milk! (Fart!)"

"How long you been a farmer, and you don't know about *Buffalo Cheese?*" (Both fall off their stools, laughing and pissing themselves…)

Pricetagg explained the procedure to the Count, whom they both found out that day was neither a Count, nor related to any royalty whatsoever. This proved imminently irrelevant and inconsequential—for now they had a New Crop they could exchange at the Fair.

Reichstag ended up financing the event, heralding banner-makers from New York and carpenters from New Jersey to build Food Stands.

159

Despite making a fortune on borscht, Pricetagg declined to offer this "cash-generator" at the 3-Day Festival, for reasons known only to himself, his id, and his super-ego.

———————————————

Whilst the "Food Fair" was a success, Spedlak's wife, Beulah-Cod, experienced dismay at her fellow Romanians, all seemingly overweight, offering nothing but fried fruits/candies at their food-stands, and lacking intellectual substance. Neither had they read James or Tolstoy, but could barely pronounce the names with a face-full of fried watermelon!

Pricetagg & the Count patented the Buffalo-Cheese, and later imported water buffalo from Romania and Italy to the English Countrysides, where they could eat fresh grass and clover grown of better quality than the home country.

———————————————

With the advent of the Industrial Revolution, the Count could mass-produce and distribute his Buffalo Cheese worldwide, thanks to Americans working 14-hour days for .03 cents a year. Furricane became rich, Reichstagg became even richer, and the world became a healthier place until World War One.

Today, the benefits of Buffalo Cheese are that it is low in cholesterol, high in protein, and serves as an excellent substitute for those allergic to Cows Milk.

Borscht, however, has been rumored to have ill-effects on women, causing them to "dyke-out" and wear short haircuts, when everyone knows that men, in general, prefer long hair in women.

11/24/2006 9:14:40 AM
Gustav Politico-Correcticanopener
Offoffmania, Romania

How "Not" to Conduct a Job Interview

During a recent marketing survey, we sent representatives from our agency to investigate hiring methods and interview techniques of prospective employers throughout Long Island. On a scale of 1-10, your company scored a negative ten (-10). In other words, you *failed*.

It is a wonder you have any employees at all, unless they are gluttons for abuse, and some people are ignorant enough to deserve it. In any event, the following critique has been prepared for your benefit, in the hope that, in the future, just as you expect your employees to meet certain standards of professionalism and productivity, that you too, may become competent enough to lead by example.

- Interview, don't *interrogate*: our reps claim that your hiring manager spoke to applicants as if they were *criminals*, and attached a negative connotation to each former job listed on their application: "Why didja leave here?" "Why didn't this job work out?" If you suspect that anyone leaving a job is doing so because of their own incompetence, you have ruled out factors such as poor treatment from past employers, a sincere desire to try something new, or personal efforts to better one's self.

- Introduce yourself at the beginning of the interview: In one instance a hiring manager began an immediate interrogation before the applicant even sat down, forcing him to *introduce himself to you* five minutes after the interview began, instead of vice-versa.

- Manager brought up "benefits" as if it were an *inconvenience*— maybe you'd rather have a sickly, unproductive workforce—the only businesses that make money off of these type of people, though, are hospitals and doctors.

- "*wha-di-ja*": hiring manager used this phrase about ten times during the course of an interview. "What did you" is the proper way to express this idea in the English Language.

- <u>"I don't want to hire someone and have them leave"</u>: Don't express fear while interviewing people. You just admitted to the future employee that you have a *high turnover*, which is hardly surprising considering what's already been mentioned so far.

- <u>Include your company's name in your advertisement</u>: Only an address was given in your newspaper ads—not much confidence/job pride exhibited here.

<u>Summary:</u>

If you don't like *people*, don't hire 'em!

Most winning companies know that *people* are their <u>most valuable resource</u>, and do their best to seek the best and keep the best. With your company's current attitude and approach, the only success you'll be able to attract will be in the following areas:

1. Losing good employees to better companies
2. Poor reputation
3. Lawsuits

Happy headhunting!

"...dah...gee, boss—duz I really haz ta (fill in the blank) AGAIN?"

—run headfirst into a brick wall—

—impersonate a dartboard—

—stop that oncoming tractor-trailer head-on with my chin—

—makes pretend I can read—

—give donations to the rich—

—sneeze in Swedish—

—count my testicles—

—test that bullet-proof condom—

—siphon gasoline through a crazy-straw—

—hose down the rhinoceros asses—

—perform open-heart surgery without a medical degree—

—play "find the micro-organism in the quicksand"—

—telemarket our "Do-it-yourself Vasectomy" kit—

—ride a tricycle in diapers in protest of lima beans—

—play Russian Roulette with a fully-loaded pistol—

—collect rare coins in other people's spare time—

—sleep in the refrigerator—

—perform show-tunes for zoo animals in a meat-suit—

—put LSD in the communion wafers—

—sleep with your wife—

"DAHHHHHHHH, O.K., BOSS!"

Diner Waiter/Waitress Etiquette Quiz

1. Rule Number One: "the customer is *always*":
    a) right
    b) overweight
    c) complaining
    d) drunk

2. Which of the following is a True Statement?
    a) all the songs on the jukebox are outdated
    b) the night shift doesn't do shit
    c) never judge a waitress by her skirt
    d) all of the above

3. The amount a customer tips you is in direct proportion to:
    a) your quality of service
    b) his/her I.Q.
    c) the amount of change stuck in between their car-seat cushions
    d) double the tax, minus tomato, over easy

4. Customers are famous for making snotty remarks. The best way to handle this snobbery is to:
    a) smile, walk away, and blow off steam later
    b) spit in their coffee refills
    c) keep bringing them the wrong order till they leave
    d) quickly slap a few band-aids on you arms during conversation, casually slipping in the fact that you're awaiting your "blood-test" results

5. You are the Diner's Direct Representative to the customer. In order to keep them coming back/ensure repeat business, you should:
    a) be courteous, polite, and always give them what they ask for
    b) spread bad rumors about neighboring/other local diners
    c) burn down neighboring/other local diners
    d) print nude male dancers/female supermodels on the place-mat puzzles

6. During an occasional lull of inactivity on your shift, you can always:
   a) help other waiters/waitresses with their orders
   b) steal each-other's tips
   c) write love poems on the back of guest-checks
   d) challenge your co-workers to another round of "hide your drunkenness from the boss"

7. Sometimes, waitresses receive unwanted come-ons from male customers. In such cases of harassment, one should:
   a) Summon the boss once he's done hitting on the other waitresses
   b) Summon a big, strong waiter after he's done flirting with the female customers
   c) Summon the power of cartoon superheroes with your cereal-box prize "activation" ring
   d) Searing hot coffee and groins don't mix well, do they?

8. Waitering/Waitressing is far from easy work, but can prove rewarding if you're willing to:
   a) keep a good attitude
   b) overcharge on the bill without getting caught
   c) work three other jobs to supplement your income
   d) quit!

New Jobs For A Hurting Economy

- Dumpster Detective
- Parking Lot Line Painter
- Classic Car Admirer
- Movie Tag-Line Memorizer
- Shopping Cart Detailer
- Stop Sign Repairman
- Amusement Park Ride Critic
- Balloon Deflator
- Slow-Food Restaurant (w/long-order cooks)
- Smoking Instructor
- Toilet-Seat Technician
- Backseat Cab Driver
- Religious Cult Coordinator
- Riot-Starter
- Bicycle Pump Inspector
- Compulsive Mystery Shopper
- Mental Assistant
- Insecurity Guard
- Motionless Detector
- Pollen-Counter

Part-Time Positions Available:

- Know-It-All (to kill conversations at parties, ruin family functions, and disrupt people in bars trying to get laid)

- Neighborhood Gossip Columnist

- Television Commercial 'Voice-Unders'

- Lost Cell Phone Retrievers

- Chronic Department Store Merchandise Returners

- Donut/Bagel Center-Hole Calibrator

- Motivational Funeral Speaker

- Divorce Planner

- Personal Experience Exaggerator

- Self-Hurt Author

- Breath Mint Tester

- Non-Profit Disorganization Volunteer

- Missing Pet Sketch Artist

- Psychotic List-Maker???

To apply for any of the following positions, please contact your local Inhuman Resources Center.

"Hospital Fun Quiz!"

Hey, gang! While you've got the free time, why not take this handy-dandy "Medical Exam" while awaiting your discharge!

1. What have you enjoyed best about your stay thus far?
   a) Giving blood and urine samples
   b) A clock on the wall that's one hour and fifteen minutes behind
   c) Pain-killer induced Euphoria

2. Instead of the hospital staff, who would you prefer serve your food?
   a) The Hooters Waitresses across the street
   b) Regis and Kelly
   c) A vending machine

3. Please choose one of the following clergy you wish to be comforted by:
   a) A priest
   b) A rabbi
   c) The Dalai Lama
   d) Voodoo Priestess
   e) The Anti-Christ
   f) An atheist

4. Does your doctor:
   a) Check in on you frequently and give you updates on your current health status?
   b) Peek his head in the doorway, pass wind, and bill you for it?
   c) Speak English?

5. Using a cell phone in your hospital room will more than likely:
   a) Disrupt normal operation of life-sustaining equipment
   b) Disrupt the lives of the people you keep calling/pestering
   c) Fuck it---no reception!

6. What in hell is that "odd-shaped diamond-tile" on the wall?
   a) An Original Pablo Picasso Copy entitled "Scrotum 1951"
   b) A Doorway to Another Dimension
   c) What happens when the carpenters go on strike

7. So far, what is the best-tasting meal you've had during your stay?

a) Plasma a la Carte
b) Intravenous Double-Whopper with Cheese
c) Water

8. Besides television, what other recreational activities would you like to see offered in the future?
a) Pin the Tail on the Anesthesiologist
b) "Mal Practice" the Clown
c) Live Doo-Wop Band "Tony B. and the EKG's"

9. One of the best-proven methods to boost the body's immune system to ensure rapid healing is:
a) Having a sense of humor
b) Frequent communication with all hospital staff
c) Frequent sex with obliging hospital staff

10. How would you rate the quality of care you have received since your arrival?
a) So fantastic I'm gonna injure myself a day after discharge just to come back!
b) I'd enjoy it more if I weren't ill
c) OK except for that "odd-shaped diamond-tile" that's freaking me out!

11. Boredom is a guaranteed "given" during any prolonged hospital stay---you can combat this "inevitable visitor" by:
a) Planning loads of activities to do once you're feeling better
b) Planning loads of activities that will make others feel worse
c) Planning to stay far away from the asshole whom made up this handy-dandy hospital quiz!

"Happy Healing!"

Note: Taking this quiz may cause Insomnia, Diarrhea, Venereal Disease, High Blood Pressure, Heart Attack, Brain Tumors, Unpopularity with Peers, Erectile Dysfunction, Immaturity, Runny Nose, Dry Eyes, Fever, Paralysis, Memory Loss, Cancer, Bad Breath, Halitosis, Bone Loss, Hair Loss, Divorce, High Income Taxes, Low Sperm Count, Uncontrolled Singing of 1970's Love Ballads from Dead Singer-Songwriters, Muscle Spasms, Headaches, Migraines, Your Grains, Everybody Grain-Grains, Blurred Vision, Rash, Psychological Instability, Layoffs, Bad Credit...

Poems
Written
Under
The
Influence
Of
Low
Serotonin
Levels

Not Too Good?

I'm feelin' weird

I don't feel right

I'm feelin' strange

(I won't be sleepin' tonight)

    Stare at the walls

    'till my eyes start to bleed

    talk to myself, and say

    "There's nothing you need"

        I think I'm mad

        I know I'm obsessed

        I can't stop my mind

        (when will it slow down and rest?)

I'm feelin' bad

Not the way that I should

My behavior is, well, let's say

It Hasn't Been Good

                I'm feelin' off

            I'm rarely on 'cue'

        Enough about me

    So, how goes it with you?

...whatever you do...

...whatever you do
don't take any advice
don't bother with maps
before a long trip

don't bother with facts
don't research/don't work
just fail, and blame it on
some other jerk!

...whatever you do
just show up and wing it
don't plan or prepare
wait 'till the last minute

don't listen to wisdom
wave off common sense
all that shit's for people
in ivory towers

...whatever you do
just ignore the Big Picture
and concentrate
on what's best for *you*—

other people don't matter
(until you're in need)
so screw these dumb fuckers
for all that they've got!

...whatever you do
don't play by the rules
if the traffic light's red
then keep on going

if the boss says "work"
find ways to screw off
if the church says "marry"
then get a divorce

whatever they tell you
is what 'not to do'
but remember, you gotta do
what's best for *you*—

when they argue, *agree*—
when they fight, *back down*—
be contrary/aggravate
just to kill time!

...whatever you do
don't design for success—
lay obstacles/booby traps,
watch others *fail!*

...whatever you do
don't question a thing
that shit's for philosophers
and folks with no life

don't wonder or worry
don't ponder/surmise
don't estimate/round off
take into account

all that shit's for those
who are paid by the hour
or raising a family
and paying off homes

▬ ▬ ▬ ▬ ▬ ▬ ▬ ▬ ▬ ▬ ▬ ▬ ▬ ▬ ▬

...so, whatever you do
is O.K., you see—
there's no consequences
(situational ethics)

vomit—curse—spit!
Pick your nose in a restaurant
Nobody cares
So just do what you please

Criticize, terrorize
Torture and taunt
Make fun of cripples
(don't forget—'blame the victim'!)

You don't need class,
Manners, or courtesy
Just become the Asshole
You were Destined To Be
Then Whatever You Do
No Matter What You Do—
You'll Be An Asshole...

...just——Like——ME!

(...pretty much says it all, doesn't it?)

Bad Ass (Too Close To Home)

We admire the tycoon
And the business exec
We worship the cutthroat
And wish we could be
Just like them…

We study the gangster
(wishing we were "that bad")
As they "drive-by" shoot
And pass out cement shoes
And we desire to Live
In Their Glamorous World…

So I find it funny
When one of these "heroes"
fires us from a thirty-year career
And screws us out of our pension
Or slits the throat
Of one of our family members
For the .29 cents
In their pocket

And I laugh my ass off, really…

But—

When
One
Lone
Disenfranchised
Soul

Straps a bomb
On his back

Or shoots 44 innocent bystanders
In a Burger King

Everybody Screams:

"How can this be?"

"What a sick world!"

"Why?"

And I laugh my ass off, really...

I've Finally Figured Out
The Secret Desire
Of Every Human Being
(Including Myself)

We All Want To Do
Whatever We Want
Whenever We Want
However We Want

We Don't Want
Anyone Else
Telling Us
What To Do

Even If It's
In Our Best Interests

We All Want
Our Own Kingdoms, Complete
With Slaves, Concubines,
Riches and Luxury

We Don't Want to Work
(And We'll Kill Anyone That Tries To Make Us Work!)

~~~ ~~~ ~~~ ~~~ ~~~ ~~~ ~~~ ~~~ ~~~ ~~~ ~~~ ~~~ ~~~ ~~~

We WANT To Kill Each Other
Because it makes us feel BIG

But VIOLENCE is a MASK
Only Hiding HURT PRIDE
Which is Much More _Intolerable_ To Human Beings
That Throwing Your Entire Life Away…

~~~ ~~~ ~~~ ~~~ ~~~ ~~~ ~~~ ~~~ ~~~ ~~~ ~~~ ~~~ ~~~ ~~~

and I laugh my ass off, really…

because human beings
are supposed to be
the most intelligent life-forms
on the planet earth

but we worship The Abuser
and sissify The Peacemaker

Until—

Until It Hits Too Close To Home.

state of affairs

Everybody uptight
Afraid to look around
To stiff to make a move
To scared to make a sound

Everybody layin' low
Nobody wanna say
What's happenin' within their mind
Afraid to lose their pay

Don't tell a joke, or turn your head
For heaven's sake, don't *laugh!*
Da cops be comin' to lock *you* up
Instead of da *real* 'riff-raff'!

The way things are? *Ridiculous!*
I ain't no 'fraidy-cat'!
I still got my 'cahones'
(and you can *quote me* on that!)

don't tell her that she looks nice
don't tell him he's not hired
make sure that all your common sense
is properly 'retired'

get rid of your opinions
and the thoughts that make you 'think'
make sure to get behind the wheel
after your 13th drink

just parrot what the neighbors say
and you'll be 'in the clear'
with nothing left inside your head
there's nothing left to fear…

(good life!)

It Must Be Nice

It must be nice
            To Have Everything You Want

It must be nice
            To Get Everything You Deserve

I don't mean to sound envious
                        I Think It's Great

Hate to sound like a jealous fool
                        But Its Too Late

It must be nice
            To Have Anyone You Want

People come and go
            But You Get To Pick & Choose

Why hide the *obvious*?
                        (I'm full of hate)

Didn't mean to spoil your fun
                        But Its Too Late

It must be nice
            To Know How To Play The Game

I wish I could
            But I'm Just Too Soft, Too Lame

Then I'd Have Everything I Want
                        And no one left to blame

Either way, I'm stuck with myself
                        a pathetic shame.

I Don't Wanna

I don't wanna play my guitar no more
I don't wanna write songs anymore
I don't wanna have to drive myself to the store
I don't wanna do nothin' anymore

I don't wanna go to work no more
I don't wanna clean the sink or mop the floor
I don't wanna pay bills or rent anymore
I don't wanna do nothin' anymore

I just wanna sit like a bump on a log
Yell "Ribbit!" on a lilypad just like a frog
Blend into the landscape and the scenery
You may find Waldo but you'll never see me!

I don't wanna fall in love anymore
I don't wanna be with people anymore
Don't give a flyin' f___ about the Superbowl Score
'cause I don't care who wins or loses anymore

I don't wanna watch TV no more
Ain't paid to think, so I don't anymore
Inhaling/exhaling just becomin' a chore
I don't want to do nothin' anymore

I may sound dejected, but I'm not, you see
I just ran outta things to do and places to be
My life is just a tape-loop goin' 'round and 'round
I ain't givin' up—

   —*Just Lookin' for a New Sound.*

Back to the Earth

It's only
A matter of time
Before

The End Will Come
And I Must Go

Back to the Earth
Where I came from

(No one lives forever…)

⸺ ⸺ ⸺ ⸺ ⸺ ⸺ ⸺ ⸺ ⸺ ⸺ ⸺ ⸺

But lately,
I've been wishing
That

I could go sooner
(why drag it out?)

There's no pleasure in this
Thinking like this
Just
Reason and Logic
Telling the Truth

I look back
On my wasted life
And think
"How could I be so dumb?"

I end up
Hating Everyone
And understanding
Nothing…

Back to the Earth
Is where I belong

Not thirty years from now
But, <u>now!</u>
Why wait?
When all I cause is hate?
(when I thought
I could make you laugh?)

I don't have
What it takes to win
I argue, but
I just give in

No one can see
My point of view
I must be crazy
Loose a screw!

I've lost
All my ability
To charm
And entertain, you see
So now
It's really up to me
To take responsibility…

--- --- --- --- --- --- --- --- --- --- --- --- --- ---

Did I try my best?
Who really knows?
Nobody cares
Even if I did

I'm feeling sorry
For myself
(like losers do
from time to time)

--- --- --- --- --- --- --- --- --- --- --- --- --- ---

Back to the Earth
Where I can rest
And stop expecting
people to

Give me the time
or listen
or say "Good job!"
or, "I think you're cool!"

I'm just a source
Of aggravation
A headache
In other people's lives

So, put away the aspirin
(you won't need it)
for pretty soon
I will be gone

And everyone
Can sigh, "Relief!"
'cause this poor bastard
took his leave

Back to the Earth
Not Heaven, Hell
Or Limbo
Or the 6th Dimension

Back to the Earth
Out of your way…

…I should have done this *sooner…*

Fuck You!

I am not in the habit
Of being profane
I prefer to be civilized
Acting humane
But as of late
It seems
Everyone's
Insane…

Overworked—underpaid
Stressed out and afraid
With nothing secure
And not really sure
Where to place
Their bets
Or
Their
Trust…

You wish you could start
The day with a smile
And enjoy your brief stay
On this Earth for a while
Grit your teeth
Bite your tongue
And go the "extra mile"…

But It Never Fails…

During the course of your day
You're bound to encounter
The Spoilers of Beauty
And the Thieves of Smiles
Who suffered Injustice
Sometime in the past
And now, it's their job
To Ruin Your Life

And the sad thing is
These Killers of Hope
With their Damaged DNA
And their Cognitive Confusion
Are slowing beginning
To Take Over The World…

They're coming to town
They're moving next door
They work down the block
In your favorite store
To infest all that's sacred
And to all you hold true
Their Mission:
To Turn Your Life Into A Zoo!

⸺ ⸺ ⸺ ⸺ ⸺ ⸺ ⸺ ⸺ ⸺ ⸺ ⸺ ⸺ ⸺ ⸺ ⸺

You wonder why folks
Slit their writs and jump roofs
You needn't look far
If you seek further proof—
The Unkind and The Rude,
The Uncaring, Aloof…

The Unreturned Love
The Bus That You Missed
The Job That You Lost
The Trousers You Pissed
The Judgement, The Critics
The Bosses, The Pain
All this aggravation
And what did you gain?

~~~~~~~~~~~~~~~~~~~~~~~~~~~~~~~~~~

The Gurus say "meditate"
Preachers say "pray"
But neither technique
Makes the hurt go away
And you Run Out of Answers
And Cute Things To Say
Till all you encounter
Are frowns everyday…

~~~~~~~~~~~~~~~~~~~~~~~~~~~~~~~~~~

For all of you folks
Who hate other's success
And who's only skilled trade
Is to Make Life a Mess
I've Just One Thing To Say
Nothing More/Nothing Less
If you saw this work's title
Then you don't have to guess…

"Fuck You!"

(Dear Reader;

I did not take pleasure in composing the following poem, nor in naming it "Fuck You".

Unfortunately, the Human Race has, in recent years, been building a rock-solid immunity against Reason and Logic. An increase in Attention Deficit Disorder hardly assists in the Lost Art of Debate. These days, in order to guarantee one's point comes across in the most uncomplicated, easily comprehended, and time-saving manner, it is now commonplace for the phrase "Fuck You" to be employed daily, and in most, if not all conversations.

Sincerely,

The Author

$$2 + 2 = 5$$

what someone once said to me in a hospital waiting room
that had never been said before:

...4 chess pieces

is all it takes

to desert a babysitting job

right smack in the middle

of making an

"Ajax Souffle"—

...they forgot to put

the "Beware of Microwave" signs up

At USC,

University of Chicago,

Which I once attended...

The Northern Thebaid

Elder Marcaruis of Optina
Read from Kontakion 12
Prophesied Future Disaster—
Warned us of the coming hell…

Let us not wait any longer
My love, we must head for the north
The others have left here already
We must set this pilgrimage forth…

I know you have doubts
As we scatter about
But I've loved you for so many years—

The Abbot of Zelenets
Tells but the truth
There's just nothing left for us here…

The desert awaits our arrival
We'll settle in, and settle down
Our worship, unhindered and quiet
The "spirit of peace" will surround…

The journey ahead is a long one
And fear greets us at every turn
But together, I know we can make it
For the Northern Thebaid we must yearn…

afterthought...

the bands that broke up
that we
want back together

the touchdown you made
back in 1982

That vacation you had
In Rio
Or Vegas

The poem you read
That revealed
All Of You

That part of your life
When nothing
Went wrong

The guitar solo
In your
Favorite song

And now you are weeping
Because
It's *all gone.*

(There's Something About The Past That's Romantic)

[There's Something About Romance That's Delusional]

{Whatever We Can't Have Is The Thing We Want Most}

romantic delusia?

My Last Day On Earth

At the end of the day

When all is said and done

After all these years

(I'm only 41)

if you were to ask me

How I wish to spend

My Last Day on Earth

Here is My Answer:

*"...all I wanna do is sit on a porch on a farm somewhere, drink beer,
and listen to bluegrass music."*

You Just Don't's Makes No Sense!

You call me up

Asking me

For my phone number—

You wrote me

A letter

Asking for my address—

"How much

Do it cost?"

You say,

"A

Dollar-

Three-

Eighty!"

I'm

Tellin'

You,

Man,

You Just Don't's Makes No Sense.

Smell
Up
And
Wake
The
Coffee

Let The Games Begin

Same Scenario
Bony-ass scarecrow
The situation is no-win
"Let the Games Begin!"

"Merning—Hi there!"
Sorry if I gave you a scare
Time to Become an Asshole Again—
"Let the Games Begin!"

Getting nowhere (getting nothing done)
Stuck on the treadmill (no time for fun)
Caught in the rat race (hook, line & sinker)
Put on my game face (you stole my line, you stinker!)

Tried to quit smoking
Lost my sense of joking
I wonder where I've been?
"Let the Games Begin!"

Can't seem to break free
Of the "powers-that-be"
And the rut that I'm in
"Let the Games Begin!"

(I need a Brand-New-Kind-Of-State-Of-Mind—
I need the Freedom to be Free—
I used to Know Someone a long, long time ago—
Re-introduce Myself to Me!)

Is my Life Ready Yet?
Think I'll "set & get"
Put a twist on the spin
"Let the Games Begin!"

It took me a while
But I caught onto their style
Now it's My Turn to Win—

"Let the Games Begin!"

Can I Have Another Beer?

Who are these imbeciles that call themselves the Human Race?
What will it take for you to see that you're a Mental Case?
Sorry—I insulted you, I must have had Too Many Beers
Pardon me, while I indulge, still more of my Subconscious Fears

Does Life Make Sense?
—I think it don't!
You say, "Attempt it!"
—I say "I won't!"
Kids, Don't Try this At Home
—Batteries Not Included
Ask me if I would like another beer
—I say, "Yes, dear!"

I'm stuck within a rerun, rut—I don't know where to go
Ain't wrote a song in years, or watched my Favorite TV Show
Will I get rich, or just replay subsistence poverty?
Will I achieve acclaim, or remain in obscurity?

What do you say?
—please repeat AGAIN! (blip)
You claim you were switched at birth
—I say, "What, then?"
You speak with half-an-accent
—Your brain needs an enema
But as for me, I'll just sit here
—and have myself Another Beer!

207

Will you be the Gal For Me (and cure me of Celibacy?)
Forever broke, or someday increase all my currency (rerun)
Please Tune In Next Week, for the answers will all become clear
As I light up another smoke and crack a lid on one more
can of beer!

━━ ━━ ━━ ━━ ━━ ━━ ━━ ━━ ━━ ━━ ━━ ━━ ━━ ━━ ━━ ━━

{<u>In Addition</u>: 4 out of 5 alcoholics surveyed recommend "drunk" for
all patrons who "lose"! (bunk)}

When Will A Man Ever Learn?

Though we were doomed from the start
You grabbed a hold of my heart
I took the bait once again
Thinkin' that I made a friend

When will a man ever learn?
No matter how his heart yearn
That all she's interested in—
Is money, ten inches and sin!

I blew my paycheck every week
For some smeared lipstick on my cheek
I sit home broke, she hits the town
I sleep alone, she sleeps around

When will a man ever learn?
That gals come back but don't 'return'
You never had her, never will
And yet, your heart is aching still

We never made it through the spring
She married my best friend, poor thing!
He's gonna give and she'll receive
He's gonna love and then she'll leave

When will a man ever learn?
Eternally his soul will burn
The phrase that ruins every life:
"I now pronounce you, man & wife!"

Oh, What A Fool I've Been!

Oh, what a fool I've been!

I tried being an atheist
I tried religion
I attempted marriage
Now I'm single again

I study and learn
But I can't seem to win...

Oh, what a fool I've been!

Tried the military
After that, civilian
Then an honest attempt
To work for a livin'

Wherever I go
It's a mess that I'm in...

Oh, what a fool I've been!

Everyone pissed off
Whenever I grin
So sit back, relax
Let the "hatred" begin!

Desiring a "good life"
Is my biggest sin—

Oh, what a fool I've been!

I wish I had learned
The "tricks of the trade"
At a much younger age
Then I'd "have it made"

Instead, I'm the bozo
Who causes upset
Who ain't found his place
In "Society" yet

While everyone wonders
"What's wrong with this jerk?"
Dreamin' his life away—
("He just don't wanna work!")

He just sits there all day
With a paper and pen
Rehashing the same shit
Again and again!

I'm still to decide
What career to begin—
Is it music or writing?
(Should I just "pack it in"?)

One day I'll get comfortable
Inside this skin—

"Oh, what a fool I've been!"

A Great 'Divide'

…it's the difference
between being
a mere
cog in
The Machine
And being
The One
Running It

It's like
Standing over a game board,
Observing all the pieces,
Carefully selecting your favorite
And saying,
"That used to be me!"

as if
a Marionette
came to life

cut it's own strings

and said,

"To Hell With You All!"

you created me

you put me here

you gave me instructions

and I followed them

but I can no longer do

the same things

over and over again

where You Win

and I Lose…

░░ ░░ ░░ ░░ ░░ ░░ ░░ ░░ ░░ ░░ ░░ ░░ ░░ ░░ ░░

they start the 'wars'
when people 'wise up'
in order to distract them
from 'quitting the game'

they just start another game
and get you involved somehow
choosing sides
'good' and 'evil'

and before you know it
there's a weapon in your hand
of your (their?) choice
and you're Ready to Kill

But—
Just a few seconds ago
You were just about to discover
The "Secret to a Successful Life"…

The Game is *rigged*

For That's All It Is—

And, once you discover

You're only just a 'pawn'

Or one of two dice

Or just a Jack of Spades (all trades?)

You Do Your Best

To Will Yourself To Life

And Escape The People

That Are 'Playing' You…

This happens to many

(It happened to me)

I refer to it

As a "Great Divide"

A chasm

A border

And once you cross over

You Can Never

See Anything

The Same Way Again.

I'm Ready To Be A "Genius" Now!

Listen Up, World
I'm coming at you
It's the latest batch of sentences
From "David Q."
Got it All Figured Out
So hear my shout—
"I'm ready to be a genius, now!"

Now, you're used to me
And my stupidity
But I've gathered up all
The Evidence, see?
I've run out of ways
To stumble and fail and
"I'm ready to be a genius, now!"

Trial and Error
For 41 years
Lotsa brain-twisting
And way too many beers
But the Powers That Be
Must have seen something in me
To permit my Survival
And Eventual Arrival—

—at the Conclusion that
I Finally Wanna Be Smart
Just like all those inventors
And the people in the Arts
No more being an asshole
(who just sits around and farts)
"I'm ready to be a genius, now!"

So set me up
In my ivory tower
And hear me spew wisdom
Each and every hour
Crowds of people will pay
For what I have to say, cause
"I'm ready to be a genius, now!"

(Are you ready for me?)

They Can't Fool Me, I'm Onto Them

(…off the top of my head—
gem
phlegm
R.E.M.
goyem
totem
poem
hem
empty (I'm on to them, see?)
femme
problem (I won't 'rob' them)
Clem
stem…
—ok, I've got enough to work with…here we go!)

They told me what I cannot do
Will you fear them, and obey, too?
I curse their heads, and spit with phlegm—
(They can't fool *me*, I'm *onto* them!)

They do not want Our Laughter Here
They'd rather see you shed a tear
I know wherefrom the Problems Stem—
(They can't fool *me*, I'm *onto* them!)

It hurts to finally see the light
They can't stand Peace, they crave The Fight
But only if we let them win
Can they continue in their sin…

217

They know that what they do is wrong
So I expose them in this song
They spoil the coal to spite the gem—
(They can't fool *me*, I'm *onto* them!)

They hate when you make Perfect Sense
Logic to them is just Nonsense
They have no heart, their heads —empty!
(They can't fool *me*—I'm onto them, *see*?)

They don't want you to figure out
Just what they're really All About
It's just One Big Conspiracy
Designed to enslave you & me…

⸺ ⸺ ⸺ ⸺ ⸺ ⸺ ⸺ ⸺ ⸺ ⸺ ⸺ ⸺ ⸺ ⸺

I'd rather remain paranoid
Than give in and become their "droid"
I rent my garment at the hem
(You guessed it, babe—I'm *onto* them!)

I said too much, I cannot stay—
For now, they're "taking me away"…
I guess that's all for this po-em!
(they can't fool *us*—we're *onto* them!)

⸺ ⸺ ⸺ ⸺ ⸺ ⸺ ⸺ ⸺ ⸺ ⸺ ⸺ ⸺ ⸺ ⸺

(Author's Note: "Sorry, Society—I did my best to "fit in".
It didn't work.)

Is There Hope For Da Human Race?

Is there hope for da Human Race?
I think so, and I think not—
It all depends on how you plead your case—
Things could go well, or end in disgrace…

We've got humanitarians & volunteers
But we've also got tyrants who stir up fears!
There's People Who Care, and People Who Don't—
There's People Who Work, and People Who Won't!

Is there hope for da Human Race?
I hope so—it's worth a shot!
You do your best wit da Time You Got
(Everybody's Goals Begin In The Same Place…)

There's potential to tap, and reasons to strive
There's goals to reach, just to prove you're alive
Now, everything we do ain't a guaranteed success
But it's better to *try*, than to *settle for less!*

Is there hope for da Human Race?
It's a question that I ponder quite a lot
Should we care for our planet, or just let it rot?
(Should I give the dog a biscuit or just spray it wit *mace?*)

We engage in cruelty, torture and war
All for fun & profit like a retail store
We steal, cheat, lie & screw our neighbor's wife
(put what you want here, reader)—You call this a *Life?*

Is there hope for da Human Race?
(The Major Drama Question of a Novel Plot)
But I really didn't mean to put you on the spot
While you were kneeling down, saying prayers & grace

219

Should we expect a "God" to save us from ourselves?
Dust off all those "Holy Books" stashed upon da shelves?
Or is it up to *us* to find the answers we need?
Should we stand still, or move our feet, indeed?

Is there hope for da Human Race?
It all depends on Which Direction We Go
It Ain't What We Know or Who We Know—

But What We *Think* and *Do*
Dat Gonna *Save Dis Place*...

"...lest the 'Q.' *Resurrect* You..."

When The World Won't Give You A Chance

...well, sometimes, Life Just Be Like Dat—
nobody holds the door or tips their hat
the birds outside refuse to sing
your doorbell and your phone no longer ring

Sometimes, Life Just Be This Way—
10 years earnings lost on One Rainy Day
Good Luck's avoiding you
There's nothing you ca do—

Chorus

When the World Won't Give You A Chance
You gotta laugh back in its face
And remind it—
That You're Still Here!

When folks won't give you a break
You gotta tell yourself it's *their* mistake
You'll lose many pearls to swine
Before you can change water into wine

So, they no longer laugh at your jokes
Your Existence seems like One Big Hoax
Don't know where your life is headed
The new day once greeted, now dreaded

Your request for a raise, denied!
The waiter brings baked chicken when you ordered fried
You find the opposite is true
Of everything everyone's been telling you

223

Chorus II

When the World Won't Give You a Chance
You gotta wave a mighty fist
And remind it—
You're still around!

When folks won't listen to reason
You may have to sit it out for a season
And while you wait your turn
Find out what you need to learn

Bridge

Dis-a-ppoint-ment, is in-e-vi-ta-ble
But, Discouragement's a *choice*
Just don't stand back—
Plan your Attack—
Make sure Da World, hears your Voice!

So, you woke up today and found
Your footing not on solid ground
You drowning in a sea
Of deadlines, aggravation, apathy

But you gotta keep on goin'
Cause it's your boat, not theirs, that you rowin'
And though you feel like you're sinkin'
Pretty soon, folks will come around to your way of thinkin'!

<u>Chorus III</u>

No, the World Doesn't Stand a Chance
Cause It Gave Up, Long Ago
No, It Couldn't
Persuade You to Quit

You beat defeat into submission
You passed the "Cosmic Audition"
CON-GRAT-U-LA-TIONS—
Your Life Starts NOW!

(he who dies with the most toys, still dies!)

END!

ADAPT AND OVERCOME

Circumstances got ya down
Life's a *Joke* and you're just a clown
Though no one here gets out alive
You must do what you must if you want to survive

Work ain't great, but it pays the bills
So what if you can only afford "no-frills"
You're earning a check and you should be proud
Someday you'll Rise Above The Crowd

The World Never Changed
Never Has, Never Will
You're constantly being
Set Up For The Kill
If you don't use the gray matter
Stuck in your head
You'll end up in the ground
It's too soon to be dead

ADAPT AND OVERCOME!

Life will push you around, and people will, too
Don't let no chump get the best of you
It seems some folks were born, just to cause others pain
Stay away from this kind, and all those who complain

Never give in, without a decent fight
If you've got rivals, you're doing something *right*!
People hate those whom they wish they could be
It's not a new concept—its called *Jealousy!*

There isn't a morsel
of wisdom in crowds
Keep to yourself, quiet!
Don't let it out loud!
It's better to listen
than to flap lips and speak
Just leave all the boasting
to the foolish and weak!

ADAPT AND OVERCOME!

Always keep something stashed in your reserve
'Cause some people just have a helluva lotta nerve
they'll teast you and taunt, just to "feel you out"
'cause they find you a "threat" to their business, their clout

People hate when you lose, people hate when you win
These double-binds we often find ourselves in
Just don't let these losers get under your skin…

ADAPT AND OVERCOME!

To Live Again

To live again—
Is nothing to be taken lightly—

To start again—
After everyone around you scatters

Folks you thought were friends

Vanish round the bend

You get the message
That they all refuse to send

⸺ ⸺ ⸺ ⸺ ⸺ ⸺ ⸺ ⸺ ⸺ ⸺ ⸺ ⸺

To love again—
When everything's been taken from you

To care again—
When the facts state only fools would do so

Thoughts keep you awake

Would it be a mistake

To take a chance again?

⸺ ⸺ ⸺ ⸺ ⸺ ⸺ ⸺ ⸺ ⸺ ⸺ ⸺ ⸺

Nobody knows just what you've been through
(And they don't have to)
Nobody has to understand

You must make The Plan
Do you think you can?
Build the strength and
Find the faith
You need to Live Again?

Nobody knows just what you've been through
(and they don't want to)
It's very rare one takes a stand

But when you do, it pays
Courage often stays
On the side of those
Who refuse to quit and get up one more time—

—to try again!
Despite the warnings from the critics
To smile again
When the world just wants you to be angry

It's a constant fight

So rest your head tonight

And prepare yourself…

To Live Again!

{Most of what we say
Just gets blown away
With the wind—
Are you listening?}

Even Now

...even then, and even now

Emotions are a roller coaster

Logic's on an even keel

And reason puts your mind at ease...

...even now, and even then

Search for Wisdom—that's the *key!*

Apply it to your daily needs

And watch how everything will *change...*

...even then, and even now

You're face-to-face with Enemies

Who destroy, 'cause they can't create

The Lives They Want, Hence: *"Ruin Yours!"*

...even every now and then

you'll find a Question begs your mind

not all of them are worth the work

of finding out the Answer...

...get to the Place where you can see

the Patterns, and the Rerun (Whole)

then pull yourself right out of it

and start to make some money.

What The Universe Wants...

It ain't up to you
And it ain't up to me
It ain't up to
Religion or Philosophy
Though we still can't grasp
What it's Purpose is yet—
What the Universe wants
The Universe gets...

If it want a preacher
It'll write you a Bible
It may want a lawyer
Who'll sue you for libel
I don't like to gamble
But on this fact, I'll bet—
What the Universe want,
The Universe get!

It make lotsa folks
Who are crippled and sick
Gave women vaginas
Equipped men with a dick
It made plants and animals
Planets, stars too!
(as if it had nothing
better to do...)

Crowds of people shout, "God!"
Other thinkers say, "Chance!"
Very few have it all
Figured out in advance
Daylight Savings Time Come
All your clocks, you reset—
What the Universe wants,
The Universe gets...

231

Take matter that's fastened
To a hot, molten core
Add six billion folks
That don't care anymore
Because they can't recall
What they're doomed to forget—
What the Universe wants,
The Universe gets!

At this point, you're thinking,
"There must be a Plan!
There must be Some Reason
For Woman and Man!"
So you draw up an outline
Your goals for success
In search of "The Answer"
To this chaotic mass-mess!

But I gave you the answer
(I said it four times!)
Surrounded by sentences
Ending in rhymes
The Universe IS
And It DOES What It DO
It Gets What It Wants—

—obviously, It Wanted _YOU._

Where
To
Send
Your
Poetry

ASSHOLIA PUBLISHING

Contact: Zig Arrette, president.

Needs: *Assholia* is a bi-monthly magazine published quarterly three times a year. Seeking poems about people who tend to piss each other off, particularly during intercourse/Bible studies. Words do not necessarily have to rhyme, but must be spelled incorrectly. Will not accept unsolicited manuscripts from non-smokers.

How to Submit: Send 2-5 of your best poems with your worst query letter. Mention personal shortcomings if applicable. Responds within 2-24 months.

Advice: *"Don't bet on the races. Floss regularly. Watch your cholesterol."*

BEEDILA-DEEDILA PRESS

Contact: Ed Ittour, editor.

Needs: Nonsense to fill in the blank pages between our advertisements.

How to Submit: "Obey someone else's authority over your own"— irrelevant to mailing us your written works for future publication, but hey, this is how *Where To Send Your Poetry* told us to format this listing.

Additional Info: Such can be found anywhere from almanacs to the internet—everyone knows this, don't they?

Advice: *"Yes, we could use some."*

CHILDRENZCHIMES

Contact: Minnie Ature, director.

Needs: Any poems and/or illustrations that are fun for children ages 4-4 ¾ and will help foster their sense of self-esteem and well-being. Recently published "Mommy and the Gynecologist" by Dr. Ty Wonnon and "Terrorists Under The Bed" by Punjeeb Leftjab Righthook.

How to Submit: Query by mail, include SASE.

Contests/Awards: "The Golden Banana Award" offered once a year to children submitting their own black & white drawings of oppressive archetypes stationed within the educational field.

DON'TEVENTRY.COM

Contact: www.don'teventry.com

Needs: We are an online fanzine promulgating themes along the likes of "quitting before you try", "abject futility", and "How To Fail In The Workplace".

How to Submit: We are not accepting manuscripts at this time, so "don't even try".

Advice: *"Read our material first. If you feel you have something to offer us, disregard the thought and go do something else. Send your works to another publisher. Prepare yourself for rejection, yet still feel surprised/ traumatized when it happens. Give up on your dreams. NOW!"*

ENCYCLOPAEDIC MISNOMER

Contact: Dick Shannary, managing editor.

Needs: Verse about people whose occupations have been "put to rest" by technology, and have had to take on new careers against their wills/lack of skills. Mr. Shannary is a former door-to-door encyclopedia salesman and goldfish trainer who has taken on the noble mission of "employing the now-unemployable" through their written works, concerning such struggles as "flipping burgers at age fifty-two" and "selling shoe inserts online".

How to Submit: Gather your best stuff in a portfolio, then hoof it from wherever you live to our front doors. Knock. Someone will answer, and then slam the door in your face numerous times until you are a bruised and bloody mess. If you're still standing after a few days, we might let you in.

Additional Info: Does not accept submissions by mail. Pays royalties in supermarket-receipt coupons.

Advice: *"Don't quit your three minimum-wage day jobs."*

FOULPLAY

Contact: Bill Uvsale, president.

Needs: Poems about famous sports figures/events throughout history, which always close out every monthly issue (included on our last page). Must be inspirational and leave the "armchair athlete" with something to think about before summoning his wife for yet another beer. Our debut issue included such works as "Babe Ruth's Babes" by George Herman, "Vince Lombardi Drinks Bacardi" by William Parcels-Post, and "Where Have You Gone, Joe Garragiola?" by Joe Garragiola.

How to Submit: Submission guidelines available in exchange for SASE or a 1973 World Series autographed baseball by Joe Namath.

GET-A-LIFE!

Contact: Sue Aside, assistant managing editor.

Needs: Bi-annual chapbook publishes works concerning those whom "wish to end it all, but don't have the guts." Needs verse designed to push these pathetic, self-pitying wastes of blood and bones out of indecision and into either 1) a life-changing epiphany, or 2) over the ledge of that skyscraper!

How to Submit: Wait until your "medication" wears off, and then send us some stuff either through e-mail or snail mail.

Contests/Awards: The "Nothing To Live For" Annual Trophy awarded *posthumously* to those writers whom (obviously) did not have the patience to endure the 4-6 week "query response" time period.

Advice: *"Don't 'kill yourself' over grammar and punctuation."*

"HUR-*HUR!*"

Contact: M. Fazeema, Founder.

Needs: This humor periodical wants *anything* that will *make people laugh!* Poems, parodies, songs, short pieces, illustrations, give us whatever ya got! We favor topics such as oversized breasts, business executives uncontrollably shitting themselves halfway through overseas business meetings, and policemen who secretly hoard cement. Nothing is off-limits! (Please, though, no more poems about circus clowns with VD—*enough!*)

How to Submit: Create something, then tie it to a brick and throw it through one of our office windows (not as easy at is sounds—we're located on the 37th floor!)

Additional Info: Pays one-time fee for publishing rights, pays nothing if we can get away with it.

Advice: *"Go fuck yourself!"* (See, that was *funny*, wasn't it? Send us some shit along these lines!)

IRONY TODAY

Contact: Mike Rofone, Editor-in-chief.

Needs: Lyrical manifestations concerning the inevitable dread experienced when one finds themselves in situations they did everything within their power to avoid: <u>Ex.—</u> getting a parking ticket while stuck in traffic court; your divorce goes through the day before your former spouse wins the lottery; a private detective who "suspects he's being followed".

How to Submit: Ironically, we are not accepting manuscripts at this time. Please try again next year.

Additional Info: We originally started out as a small newsletter entitled "The Predictable Preamble", containing short stories that readers had 'figured out the endings to' after the first paragraph. Ironically, it sold amazingly well, for it made our "not-so-intelligent" fan base feel like geniuses once a month. We spun our small profits into the stock market and re-organized our content to attract a more literate/snob-infested audience.

JUST POEMS

Contact: Al Cohall/Mary Wonna, editors.

Needs: *Just Poems* excepts poems and *poems only*! Over the years, we have been inundated with short stories, novellas, drawings done on toilet paper, photographs of tree bark, and solicitations from level-headed atheists. We have been listed in this directory for the last three years, and you folks still don't get the message, do you? Send us *poems!* This is why Mary and I started this periodical—to present great literature to the world! We know you're out there, poets! *Please!*

How to Submit: Send copies only, not original works. Manuscripts sent to us will not be returned. Will pay ten percent royalties rapidly if we can get some 'actual poetry' sent to us, and not all this other 'miscellaneous hullabaloo'!

Additional Info: Nothing else to add here except that if we continue to receive anything other than verse, we're both packing it in to go live on that commune in Vermont.

KNOWLEDGE AND WISDOM MAGAZINE

Contact: International Press Office, Washington, D.C.

Needs: This quarterly magazine is dedicated to the research of workable and applicable anecdotes, parables, precepts, quatrains, and platitudes past and present, sifted from various backgrounds and cultures around the world. We are dedicated to the enlightenment of the human race, and will accept those works that inspire people to 'step up' and 'make this a better existence' for humankind now, as well as subsequent generations.

Needs? Oops! Sorry about that, we tend to ramble a bit sometimes… "K & W" usually finishes at about 199 pages, with minimal advertisements. We feel it is in the best interests of our readers and anyone who "craves wisdom" to get the most for their hard-earned dollars. We try to pack the most and the best of contemporary authors in between our pages. Research is—

NEEDS! Please pardon us—We think we were supposed to be listed in the "Author's Market", not here! We don't accept poetry, just well-researched and historically based…

LET'S FAIL! DIGEST

Contact: Global Press Office, Washington, D.C.

Needs: "Self-sabotage" is the tantamount theme toted herein—we are looking for short, medium, or long poems having to do with people ruining their own careers, relationships, or health, right at the pinnacle of personal success.

How to Submit: Call us on the phone and recite your poem live to one of our apathetic operators.

Additional Info: Also seeking pieces about folks who "deliberately block others from achieving victory, unwittingly hold others back from progress, & senselessly get in the way of other people's lives and daily routines".

Contests/Awards: Since when does anyone give prizes out to 'losers'?
Advice: "Who cares if one is *always* a loser? It's more interesting to see someone *almost-win*, and then, *forfeit it all* because of some stupid character defect!"

MONEY FOR RHYMES

Contact: Goast Rhiter, publisher.

Needs: *Money For Rhymes* is a company that helps already-established poets get through 'writer's block' by contracting unknown/unpublished amateurs to write in their styles and produce product for them during 'dry periods'.

How to Submit: Query first, with SASE, to see which authors we will need you to imitate. We will send you some past 'sample' works of 'currently-impotent' poets, and then, see if you can 'whip up some magic' and get back to us within three months or less.

Additional Info: This gig pays well, but, unfortunately, you get no "writer's credits" or royalties, just a one-time lump sum in a paper bag you'll have to come pick up from our bookkeeper, Rocco, out here in Detroit, if you're able to make the trip.

Advice: *"By providing this service, you are enabling hundreds of once-marketable writers pay their rent and sustain their drinking habits. Everyone has to get their start somewhere, and, who knows? YOU may be the starving poet one day, in need of our services!"*

NO CHANCE IN FUCKING HELL PUBLISHING

Contact: E. Pluribus Scrotum, CEO.

Needs: Poetry and short stories about the 'self-deceived', who hold fast to the irrational belief they are going to "make it big" as authors someday. Themes must be centered around and about "eventually accepting reality", "finding suitable/sustainable employment", and "leaving writing to the truly talented/gifted".

Please Don't Send:

- Light Verse
- Inspirational Poetry
- Illustrated Poetry
- Mushy
- Self-pitying
- Confessional
- Boring
- Indulgent
- Teary
- Unrequited Love Poems
- Amateur/irrelevant
- Rhymed poetry
- Devotional Verse
- Rhyme/Meter seem to be of major importance
- Craft for it's own sake
- Classical Poetry
- Typewriter Poetry
- Concrete Poetry
- Surrealism
- Doggerel or 'greeting card verse'
- Unedited work
- Cliché
- Anything incomprehensible/too derivative
- Spoken word
- Slam
- Rap Poetry (if it does not translate well to the written page)

- Predictable rhyme
- Monotonous rhythm can also be a problem
- Sonnets
- Political
- Religious
- Experimental
- Shock
- Novelty
- Overtly Sexual
- Poems with trite concepts or meaning dictated by rhyme
- Florid rhymed verse
- Collections without purpose
- Purely aesthetic, precious, self-involved poetry
- Traditional
- Obscene
- Foreboding
- Graphic gore
- Violence
- Overly sentimental
- Horror
- Gothic
- Pet related
- Humor
- Science fiction
- Previously Published
- Narratives about family
- Simplistic verse
- Annoying word hodge-podges
- Preachy
- Inconsistent meter
- Forced rhyme
- Stream of consciousness
- Avant-garde
- Esoteric
- Academic
- Didactic
- Speculative

- Erotica
- Explicit language
- Violence
- Scholarly
- Critical
- Outlandish
- Lengthy
- Long-winded
- Message-oriented
- Genre
- Serious
- Straightforward
- Ranting
- Swearing
- Metrical schemes
- Abstraction
- Teenage angst
- Sermons
- Obscure
- Only has meaning to the writer
- Seasonal verse
- Whining
- Pissing
- Moaning
- Free verse
- Trite rhymes
- Vulgarity
- Nature poetry
- 'bubba' poetry
- Introspective
- Sloppy hipster jargon
- Improvisatory nonsense
- Handwritten
- Sentiment
- Musing
- Poor quality
- Profane

- Juvenile
- Relativism
- Hackneyed versifying
- Poems typed in all capital letters
- Death
- Aging
- Illness
- Helpless/hopeless
- Falsely sweet
- Sophomoric
- Sing-song verse
- Formalist
- Self-Indulgent
- Formulaic
- Tree poetry
- Dense language
- Gushing
- Lists of emotions
- Anything that displays an ignorance of modern poetry
- Earthquake poetry
- Cute bunny poems
- Knee-jerk
- Naïve rhymers
- City punk
- Corny
- Fluff
- Syrupy
- Gibberish
- Meta-poetry
- 'Based-on'
- Self-absorbed
- Riffs off of other famous writers
- Mainstream
- Sainted granny garbage
- Limericks
- Epics
- 'dashed off'

- Maudlin
- Syllabic
- Whimsical
- Fanciful anecdote
- Modern
- Formless
- Existentialist
- Staid
- Generalized
- Topical
- Broken-prose
- Cloying
- Conventional imagery
- Compulsive article-droppers
- Butterfly
- Saccharine
- Rambling pseudo-beat poetry
- Dum-dum rhymes
- Name dropping
- Untitled poems
- Never-before published authors
- Unfresh
- Sure-of-itself
- Song lyrics
- Blatant rhyme
- Classical
- Poems that 'tell'
- Blasphemous
- Atheist
- First-drafts
- Pretentious
- Translations
- Extremist
- Long pieces
- Short pieces
- Middle-sized pieces
- Fiction

- Non-fiction
- X-rated
- Taboos
- Egotistical
- Satanic verse
- Pointless obscenities
- Anything with an agenda
- Stale metaphors
- Uncertain rhythms
- Lack of line integrity
- Private symbolism
- In-process work
- Flat-statement
- Workshop hackery
- Children's poetry
- Adult poetry
- Senior poetry
- Middle age poetry
- Outer space alien poetry
- Illegal alien poetry
- Scatologic language
- Tripe
- Topical
- Unsure of why it was written
- Neurotic soul-bearing poetry
- Watered-down surrealism
- Flippant
- Prurient
- Poetry written without thought
- Internet poetry
- *Satire or parody…*

Epilogue:
"I
Free
The
World"

So nice of you
To read this book
And take an adventure
Through my world-view

You may feel the same
Or totally different
About all the things said
In this brilliant collection

And if
I've made you
Think
Or
Feel
Or
Learn something
You didn't know before

Or ignited in you
A pure desire
For a Better World
(Than the crap we're handed)

And even if
I pissed you off
(as I'm wont to do
with folks 'off the page')

Then guess what, friend?
I've Done My Job!
The Only Thing
I Know How To Do

Take Information
Assimilate it
Analyze it
Spew it back out
On the printed page

And hope for the best
That 'others' exist
Who share the same 'brain-waves'
Enjoy the same thoughts…

But you know what?

I'm Not Always Right
Just Because I Write

I make mistakes
Just like Everyone Else

And though I vie
For a Better World

Sometimes I'm the Bozo
Who upsets others

And causes them
To reach for a pen

And document the pain
That I handed them

In the hope that others
Will relate to their feelings

And all group together
To avoid cement-heads like me

Yes, we all
Want the World
To Be Made
In Our Image

But if everything
Were, in fact, all the same
Who'd end up the 'scapegoat'?
Who could we 'blame'?

When things go wrong
(as they're wont to do)
and we can't get past
our own anger and rage

No, sir!
Surely we
Can't Blame Ourselves!

〰 〰 〰 〰 〰 〰 〰 〰 〰 〰 〰 〰 〰 〰 〰

In any event
(as my uncle is wont to say)
I'm just taking the time
To let you know

That sometimes I 'nail it'
And sometimes, I'm 'off'
Sometimes, I just write it
To make you all laugh!

So my answer to all
Who want a Better World
Is that sometimes, a laugh
Is the best we can do

But we can't always smile
Sometimes, life just ain't funny
In any event—
Smile Anyway…

(Dear Reader: You are Now Free from the shackles of the "David Q.
World-View". Please create a more hopeful one for yourself.

Sincerely,

D.Q.T.)

Special Thanks To...

- The Gang at iUniverse: For the *obvious*.

- Everyone Who Broke My Balls Between The Years 1966—2009: Your personal initiative provided the inspiration for half, if not most, of the material included herein.

- 5-HTP (5-Hydroxytryptophan): The new dietary supplement (vitamin) that assists in the manufacturing and distribution of the proper levels of *serotonin* across the blood/brain barrier, necessary to prevent one from becoming a *full-blown asshole*.

This book is for *Everyone Else Who's Got It All Figured Out*, just like me.